The Other Harmony
The Collected Poetry of Eli Mandel

— VOLUME 2 —

The Other Harmony
The Collected Poetry of Eli Mandel

— VOLUME 2 —

edited by
Andrew Stubbs
and
Judy Chapman

CANADIAN PLAINS RESEARCH CENTER
2000

Canadian Plains Research Center
University of Regina
Regina, Saskatchewan S4S 0A2
Canada
Tel: (306) 585-4758
Fax: (306) 585-4699
e-mail: canadian.plains@uregina.ca
http://www.cprc.uregina.ca

Canadian Cataloguing in Publication Data

Mandel, Eli, 1922–1992.

    The other harmony : the collected poetry of Eli Mandel

    (University of Regina publications, ISSN 1480-0004 ; 6)

    Includes index.
    ISBN 0-88977-138-3

I. Stubbs, Andrew James.   II. Chapman, Judy Lea, 1954–
III. University of Regina. Canadian Plains Research Center.
IV. Title. V. Series.

PS8526.A52 A17 2000   C811'.54   C00-920144-0
PR9199.3.M347 A17 2000

Cover Design: Donna Achtzehner, Canadian Plains Research Center.
Cover Photo: Don Hall, University of Regina.

Photos for *Out of Place* (Volume 1, pages 235 to 300) courtesy of Ann Mandel.
All other photos taken near Estevan, Saskatchewan, by Don Hall, University of Regina.

Printed and bound in Canada by
Houghton Boston, Saskatoon, Saskatchewan

Printed on acid-free paper

TABLE OF CONTENTS

VOLUME 2

DREAMING BACKWARDS 535

from *Trio*

from *Fuseli Poems*

from *Black and Secret Man*

from *An Idiot Joy*

PREFACE

This is Volume 2 of *The Other Harmony: The Collected Poetry of Eli Mandel*. Volume 1 contains the editors' Foreword, *Trio, Fuseli Poems, Black and Secret Man, An Idiot Joy, Stony Plain, Mary Midnight, Out of Place*, and *Life Sentence*, together with notes for the poems in Volume 1. Volume 2 contains three books of poetry—Mandel's contributions to *Third Person Singular*, and the selected volumes *Crusoe* and *Dreaming Backwards*—as well as eighty-two uncollected, unpublished poems, notes for the poems in Volume 2, and two indexes: an index of the first lines of the poems from both volumes and an index of poem titles from both volumes.

OTHER COLLECTIONS/ VERSIONS

THIRD PERSON
SINGULAR

Experience

There was a house and a boy;
And one to whom the shy fingers of day were exploring pirates
Was a passionate actor, who by night and in shadows
Completed the plot, acting from crisis to crisis;
His own prompter for the missing lines.

Within such exceptional walls from scene to scene
He went acting, to whom the faultless winds
Were a favorite script, the sun,
Through the pasteboard trees of his memory,
A fine stranger to melt and murder snow.

A border land, a strange frontier
With new stars, a baby moon that stared
And in the sky propounded impossibilities....
Where the soft explosions of spring on a warm front
Puzzled his breath and with bright new tools
Banged at the old plumbing of his heart;

And the green sea, time, lapped at his small geography.

For houses are only islands and are flooded,
The one tree grows wave-weary, the gulls
Flutter and follow the tall ship to sea....

and the unreal dead gather spitefully
to betray the living and the former absence of history,
argue with a child's brain
and a child's game.

The Lab Assistants

In the morning they decide, legitimately, to awake;
Eyebrows turned back, and shaved
To the consistency of fawn leather,
The young men severally adjust their smocks,
Their ties, their shoes and minds—
Equating the ionic values of their world.
And I have seen the shell-rimmed electrons
Circling the neutral orbits of their eyes.

Each day they apply with neat starched fingers
The adequate lesson; their trade makes
A chemical decision of their face...
Reflects: "The segment measured, weighed
And balanced, interpolate a decimal and with care
Solve for uncertainties."
                    Then, stuffed like a very large owl,
They sit unblinking with a glass-eyed placidity
On the shelf of my intense and wonderful
Confusion.

Wherefore yon sun and the youthful music of the lily
Troubles my gaze (Thy slim young body perhaps,
And thy flaxen limbs) and a hoard of ancient things,
—ere life eke everlasting did befall—
Sweet Thames, makes poetry, until I end my song
creeps in between their split-second answer and
unbalances the equation
                    undoes
the startled mathematics of my heart. He spoke
and down he fell.

Letter for a New Year

Standing in the heart of darkness or silence,
In the cathedral of broken trees, in the rain,
You sang to me, my German girl, your long blond hair
Like the whips of your booted boy whom I had killed,
Who killed my Jewish cousin. "Ich liebe diche."

Now the student, clothed in old journeys,
Visits in familiar places; carefully
Retards his anguish and allows his soul
To stretch from page to page, the cover of a book.
And the great plains are as dear as his mirror
To discover from Europe, a blankness on a silver shine.

Given to long appraisal and the soft assertion,
Whispers of slant argument and dialectic honour,
Grows pale if his dreams will threaten
To dynamite at all costs
Through rocks to wells bursting with oil.

Europe is not here. How can we be given to great praise?
Remember the fallen, crying, "I am the forward half
Of your time, why let me go?" We shall go
Blind, hollow and stagger through streets yet
Since we languish; crying dirty tears at our death,
Not the celebrated black and white death of great men.

So we have done it twice, faith of our fathers.
Our blood turned to patriotic fire, flared
With brief mischief, tugging the quick trigger;
One blossom exploded the night,
Made a flash photograph of our passion,
Then left December alone with snow and skin.

And the student of manners, of good conduct,
And citizenship, readjusts his ruffled
Canadian passion like a professorial robe;
Reports in his thesis; Europe
Is a country of cathedrals.
I have visited Cologne.

While blood booms back and forth a quartered message still,
Moves also to learning, questions the dialectic of
The broken cathedral of trees
Where the blond aryan girl and the dead Jew stretch arms
Like crosses to the rain; "Ich liebe diche."

Therefore let us present to the student
With his thesis on morals, in his hands
The fabulous future, while the rain falls
Impartially on all the plains and on the cathedrals.

Poem

Strange inhuman brothers who won't hear
How this begging wind has hissed a large
Exigency. Stopped like a gibbet by a rose
Or garden, they won't hear how it begs
From the church, begs from the shopkeeper,
Begs from a kiss. Never so angry as a kiss
My heart skips like a muffled drum,
Shaking its way through anxious skin
Like thieves housebreaking on the moors,
The last street, the last house
And a stale and starving room.

The war has taught me to conceal
The frantic posture, cracking of limbs,
Cracking of trunk and heart.
But the trees still stretch in the queer frost.
The blood gathers black and congealing.
The crashed and splintered arms,
An angry face cut in the snow like stone,
A cross, claw at that wind's broken brain.

The Age Has Reason for Its Age

Baudelaire's women, like flowers, wind around my dream;
Some fondling dwarfs, some skeletons, some ancient men.
The skies are opened; in a rushing stream
Demoniac figures plunge and dance like rain.

Crude verses crazy poets fling at me and laugh;
A lewd and profane balladeer makes song
Into a passion play to frighten Christ,
And Passion, in a long low gown, plays
Coyly in a chair with an orange cat.

"Christopher," I say to the bearded man;
In a pensive mood, he thinks
While stars expire faintly as a breath;
"Christopher, my friends are dancing here,
The dance is long, though Time is just a dwarf.
Time limps, Time drags a broken leg,
Come join the dance; regale us with a song."

Carefully butting his cigarette, he rose;
Walked from the corner, adjusted his lapel.
Ah, now the sadness and the gentle look,
I thought, "FORGIVE THEM," perhaps
His quiet voice will say;
One savage look at all the crowd he throws.
Took Passion, danced with Her,
And in the morning
Quiet, he walked away.

Afternoon in a Cafeteria

The hour splits, and half-unseen
Trails its black fragments through our words.
We ignore time and restless in our dream
Let minutes wind like violins, weird
In the smoke of cigarettes around our heads.

One, half aware of the world outside
Looks up cautiously to eye the thing,
Certain to be frightened if I said,
"There the stranger plays upon his string
In his blue ariettes around our heads."

If I should chance to say, "There,
In the midst of coffee cups and butts,
The invisible song curls like a hair,"
Time and our coffee would explode;
We might be left just anywhere;
The world might end.

The hour comes together; its black hulk hangs
Dog in the corner, like a hoax,
A sad St. Bernard perpetrated on our afternoon.
We console its presence with a joke.

Ulysses

I wonder what Ulysses thought as he set out,
Close to the legendary isle; lips set and firm,
Beard curled and brave upon the sea;
What subconscious whirlwinds twirled beneath that brain,
Knowing of personal dangers such as we evade.

Think of him pacing his deck no wider than a room,
Eyeing the sea for dragons, suspicious of a smile or song
That might, clever were the sirens, turn a man to pig.

He must have lived in separate thought than us,
Who would wax the ears of sailors.
I think he who had slaves knew what enslavement meant.
He could have let them be skinned on that island.
But his eye fixed on a prophecy, wife weaving the story,
Lashed to a mast, a wheel, he let the boat go on
Rocking in the classic pattern of an old sea.

The Minotaur

It happens easily when the light flares around you
And you are gay in the warmth and easy sun
With admiring friends hung round like mirrors;
You are given a string and sent winding
Where walls and paths roar with vagueness.
The taut string springs final warning down your nerves
And you are out in the labyrinth, an unbelieving sacrifice.

Round the last corner the vast arena spreads
The terrible circle, and your eyes go to the centre
Where the beast raises his slow head,
The bull neck, the horns and spreading nostrils;
Crouched on his carnage alone with the bones of men.

Holding your string you prepare for his rage.
His small eyes meet yours and you grow hot with his violence.
How he hates in the labyrinth and grows rage with murder
Into a garden of white bones, piling white bones
Into a jumble of gleams in the bad glare of a white sun.

Always you face the beast with his rage of killing
And he hates, being alone, in the terrible centre;
Wearing his task, tearing the cloth of man,
Adding by year youth and the gay light.

Always the string leads you back
To belief and the better world, but you are gone
From the time when light flared around you
With a gay wash of warmth and an easy sun.

Poem

How else should I praise the heart's excellence in season?
Erect art with handsome grass, the imagination
Stones logic to silence and daggers into reason.

Else winters us into drifts and ruts;
Skeletons our hands; draws the skin tight
And skulls the face with tips of horrid thought.

How else should I do it but love the sea of me
Which waters the sight and by waves makes
The ghost of my coastline hard-sanded and free;

The crooked ghost of past and lost time
Candling its flame through wax and melted me?
How else honour the fame that lives through mine?

Not surely save praise or start a heart
For the wreath-bearers, sorrowing their grief
And salting it with envy of their hurt;

If not envy, then what bequest unrolls
From their careful tears placed on the earth?
That death act tombs and carves beneath my soul.

What other honour is to man but with laughter?
Youth does it by staring at cripples,
Endures, and pins merriment on the weak and bereft

Or only the older; by staring too long can braze
The eyeball to stone and still to chill marble
The long strokes of death's eraser,

By wishing, waste the eager leap of time to sun,
River the blood into a driving stream,
Unshadow and make statement into man.

The Sleep-Walker

Here he took a flower, touched to the soil
A superstitious finger, and here a cup of snow;
Patterned those diamonds to his slow awakening
And aching nerves, like flakes, left on the cloth
The broad stain of a wet and melting spot.

Walked in a windstorm and listened to doctors
Probing the nervous tendons; blocked the wide doors
With bolts to hold desire and make the grey
Academy a world with paths, walls
Gardens and a room to study.

Occurred in the burnt pattern of his heart
The ashes, folding their arms, stubborn and insistent
Like pain, raining steadily in even sheets,
His steps, stunned to a motionless walking
And his sleep-talk made neither poem nor wit
For the classic severity of science.

Not able to touch in his brown dream
The clean awakeners pushed him to daylight,
Urged their merry action and mummery
Upon him, like the sun, forcing his eyes
To fly open from his closed fantasy of love;
Speaking of their virtue together and to him

Of what flimsy architecture he had built in
Fervid darkness, trying new lines without sight.
But the sleep-walker turned from their bright
Congratulations, and was left in a corner
Grieving his dream, the perfect mourner.

Song

"Who is the puppet, and who the puppeteer?"

Through drifts and snow, steps fumble in a path.
The puppet moves and clicks along the walk.
In a dance, the people are moving through the park
Along the streets, dancing, where ice and colored signs are sharp.

Snow muffles sound and you can't hear the dance.
The puppet lifts a wooden face and sings.
The lights go on and off; the audience applauds
With one sharp stroke, leans forward,
Separates the strings.

The wind lifts up, a vein of snow trails out.
The puppet laughs and laughs into the snow.
A pale and absent smile is hung along the street
Where figures move and dance, and in the colored lights
Inhuman faces glow.

Now Who Will Celebrate

Now who will celebrate the aged, ungracious queen,
Romance, the fleet of ships born from her eyes?
Helen is ancient now, the paint wears thin.
That smile is grown crooked as a lie.

Note how the wrinkles creep beside her eye,
Swelling like flowers after heavy rain.
The celebrated goddess has been raped
And rape repeats a prelude in her brain

And yours. This is how poetry begins,
Drumming a little, saccharine, in your mind;
Repeats: Helen is old. Helen is very old.

Love Song

Gladly we watch the red and ready sun
I and the girl who walks along with me.
The sky turns whiskey-sour, the night comes on.
Watching the night she is prepared for me.

We walk, whisper, the stars appear.
A spanish guitar amors the world for her,
Plucking at sentiment in drops like tears,
Burning at each drink, adroit but furred.

Carry this soap opera fifteen minutes to the end,
The sponsor has a few words to say before we're through
A short pause for identification then you
May go on with whatever you choose to do.

So the stars wheel twice around her brain
Run madly into comets, burst and flare.
In the courtyard I leave her, in the morning
I leave, on a paved and marble-patterned stair,
Standing with flowers and moonlight in her hair.

Time like a dope-fiend takes a powder
Runs stupidly in the quiet air, grows old,
Grinning from painted lips to pointed ears.
The last house of cards collapses, the deck is cold.

The Lover

In a room where everyone is neat and starched
He comes in like the wet laundry;
His bedraggled soul unwraps like an unpressed sheet
And flaps at the ordered people, who, being polite,
Avert their eyes from somebody else's wash.

(Coasting in on his head at full sail
He watches eternity in every second;
From the bow of his clipper he hollers
Like the wind...
"I look for you always, always.")

Oh he is unstarched, unpressed and sodden.
Machines have been turning him over and over
Slapping his sides and his soul;
While she, inadvertently, switches the power to full
And grinds him in a wringer till he's done.

Hung like underclothes on the line of her person
He struggles in a wind which he beautifully creates.
No one is noisier, more violent, so attached;
She holds him easily with the clothespins of her smile.

While he suffers on the line, in his own wind,
He is smiling at the unlovely people
Who have finished with laundry.
Where the sun of her body comes out to dry him,
He steams in the air, in her brightness he's shining.

To a Lady Who Danced the Spanish Dances When the Room Was Dark and Snowlight Fell from the Cold Window

The room became a stage.
Lights fixed and spotted from snow
beamed long and across
a tense and accurate audience
leaning forward with critical eyes.

You became stern and attentive.
Denied the public and exacted passion
from the composer; sang to him,
caressed his face and closed
his poor mad eyes with talented fingers.

The madness of being one thing and its target
seized the crazy poet who laughed to himself
and sang with your arms and your long body

While the soft long town of music came about you
and you went farther and farther down the streets
searching with your high gentle eyes
for a field where dawn is and music ends

And the poet cried because you were going
down the streets and along the hills
farther and farther away from him
wrapped in your music like a Spanish shawl.

To a Lady Who Acts

You bring a delicate, precise, emotion to the house.
Around you the supporting cast turns and genuflects.
The tableau takes form and built over bodies
You arise, stretch carefully exquisite hands
And register the final tragedy.

Such watersnake emotion writhes throughout the act.
In pattern ah very like the script, hearts come
And kneel to you and fall.
Your quiet voice trembles and pronounces
In the most exact diction, Love,
Bearing its passion like a golden box.

As gracious as a queen you accept the burden
(heavy though it is)
And deep in cool water, sail graciously away,
Trimming your canvas like a small Egyptian craft.

My voice stammers wickedly under stars
Watching you go, while down from that sky
Dreams come pattering, raining in my eyes.

To a Lady in a Dark Corner

Belted, uncouth and black as the evening,
Which like an uncowled monk, comes
Treading his destructive path through afternoons
To an alcoholic sunset untidily spread like wine,
Excommunicate and unfrocked, I shall go on loving you.

Also despite that Heathcliff's damaged, darkened soul
Is somewhat beyond me, moor-bound and savage
As that twisted tree, I will pursue my love,
Humourless and grim; Envy the shadows
That may cup and hold with eloquent embrace
The deepened hollow and curve of your cheeks;
Declare my eyes are fork-tongued serpents
Flickering a green anger at the wind that moans
About you and traces with its fingers
Instead of mine, your extravagant delicate features.

Dawn will find me maintaining a deliberate frown;
Scowling at the intense fragility and good taste
Of morning's approach which like a gentleman's
Agreement bows in a polite company.

So to all things courteous and pleasant,
Manners, the accepted graces, chivalry
And the public mores, I shall be exile;
Expressing a profound, discourteous jealousy
And an ugly mood. (And never again be seen
In the pagan charms of Attic temples;)
Pursuing my course among the Gothic arches,
Fixed on the church wall with an angry face,
Gazing down at your elegance in the courtyard
Or the corner, where you accept the courtesies
Which will inevitably be yours; while my love for you,
A pig-iron dragon, stares with its gargoyle eyes.

Operation "Love"

(The amputation was a success;
since I will have none of you,
I leave you some of me.)

Asceptic, my doctor smiles down at me again
Who am his patient rising from that dream
Where ether stuffed a suffocating palm
Across my mind, and the instrument separated
The amputee from his limb.

Brain stops reeling in the double dream.
World focusses again.
A nurse with a cool hand
Measures a recovering pulse,
Whispers a word and is gone.

Solemn and sacred at my feet, like the arm that is gone
Lies a small love; attendants will arrive
And carry it out on a platter that is man.

Convalescent, I take my single-handed soul
In its one grip, learning to live lop-sided
And do with a hand and a hook
What two arms have done before.
Since I believe that hands are so great
A part of love, I will be able
To love others with only half of me now.

Sunday Night

Wind patterns snow in old arrangements,
Trees know, acknowledge and accept.
The universe is a soft light brush of hair, tonight.
The universe brushes softly in your hair.

I, who in April, sang a little while
Will sing no longer
When the snow is on your hair tonight
And on your dead lips, the wind
Is kissing snow much softer
Than the hollows of your throat or palm.

Shall I wear black tonight and scowl?
You are gone. The universe still brushes
Softly in the long hair of the night;
In trees, in stars,
My little dreams expire.
The wind is kissing snow
Much softer than your lips, tonight.

I have heard no cries, no wild sobbing.
None tear at clothes or spread their hair with ashes.
The universe is beautiful, my love.
The few gone mad are mad
But not of love.
The sane will wander about a little while longer,
Staring in mirrors, asking about memories,
And finally in all their rooms, gone white as an aspirin,
Will clutch their stiff hands to their breaking skulls.

The wind is kissing lips
And patterns snow tonight.

Ars Poetica of E.W.M.

You will wonder, Voltaire, that a young man
Scarcely twenty
Can fret over his verses…

A bird studying music;
Grass with a notebook on "How to Grow."

Not do high deeds and not fret over dying,
Or say, "reason enough has been in the singing."

With poor Pound mad in Italy,
Where beauty's broken window
Scants and tilts in the sun.

CRUSOE

in the dark wood, a way

Crusoe

1

Greek men dance alone.
The Hebrew yells at stone.
Others eat glass.
Name your own vice, Englishman.

2

The snail's trace:
doubtful words.

Do not ask how I have come
to an exact madness
or what my keepers name
the frenzy of compliant sense.

The dancer alone in his dance
utters the terrible sound of his limbs.

3

This was written for a foundling,
alien, Greek, Hebrew,
to the memory of my sane parents,
in order not to go mad,
and for my keepers' sake,
that I might learn
singular love

no other is to blame.

Minotaur Poems

I

It has been hours in these rooms,
the opening to which, door or sash,
I have lost. I have gone from room to room
asking the janitors who were sweeping up
the brains that lay on the floors,
the bones shining in wastebaskets,
and once I asked a suit of clothes
that collapsed at my breath, and bundled and
crawled on the floor like a coward.
Finally, after several stories,
in the staired and eyed hall,
I came upon a man with the face of a bull.

II

My father was always out in the garage
building a shining wing, a wing
that curved and flew along the edge of blue air
in that streamed and sunlit room
that smelled of oil and engines
and crankcase grease, and especially
the lemon smell of polish and cedar.
Outside there were sharp rocks, and trees,
cold air where birds fell like rocks
and screams, hawks, kites, and cranes.
The air was filled with a buzzing and flying
and the invisible hum of a bee's wings was honey
in my father's framed and engined mind.
Last Saturday we saw him at the horizon
screaming like a hawk as he fell into the sun.

III

They chose among us in the fall of the year,
by lot, behind fierce masks designed of sign
to ward off the imminent descent of the sun people;
someone talked of a dying god, as if
the young ones among us believed in
that any more, others cautioned us against the voices
we were always supposed to hear and these
were stubborn about the women crying.
I remembered the face of one who brought me here
when they drew my name in the hall,
it was her persuasion in the beginning,
something about fathers.
                              Like the others before me,
I saw only their breasts that appeared on the walls,
legs moving in unison, the swaying of sweat-stained
bodies and their half closed eyes:
all the talk about signs when I knew
the boys were only waiting for the
women to undress, as they always did,
                              snickering
and those same fields that make a dawn in vision
where birds begin to live in rocks and screams.
It is hard to feel free of accusation
because of eyes
although there is a difference between revelation
and action bellied into life, between
believing in voices
and knowing the chances that we have to take.

IV

Now I am dressed in a multitude of rooms
like a Chinese box, and slip from covers
into covers   Dawn will not help me nor
the day's exposure   I am a prodigious pun
to hide and show myself between these walls
this otherwise where sunlight
dressed in a tweed suit pursues me
or a stranger in the rooms
          and footfalls on the stairs
and eyes   and over all
     the whispering and chattering of the walls
          the pipes and hammered arteries of the place.

Is that a revelation in a field of light
competing with a shadow on the rock?
A bird's shadow seen from here?
Or a cloud between the sky and land
footed and patterned into phrases?

It is hours since I have been in here.
If I had once seen anything
except birds,
rocks, land, and all winter long
                    the ice and snow

V

Within these walls I am to look for light
Or hold an abstract in my hand as firm
As apples or the golden bar the older men
Returned to us. Remember that. That spring
There were those crowds and crowds below the cliffs
This side of town and all along the beach,
Flags out, booths filled with toys, and one,
The better salesman of the lot, a beggar
From the north had miniatures of bars
That went like hotcakes. Fleece for the crowd.
A replica to keep you as it kept our men
This winter past. Then noise, flocks wheeling overhead,
The painted ship, a bauble on the sea, came like a toy
To harbour.
                    And the tall bronzed men descended
Between the cheers and speeches at the harbour mouth,
Talk about campaigns in lands we'd never heard of,
Cheers and lewd remarks and laughter, the look
In other eyes, and counting of the crew
And stooping at the gaps aghast.
That was another death, the shock in surf,
The rock's point of view, the hawk
Momentarily composing before the fall
His target of a landscape from the sky.
The trailing plume before the dark.
Night on the beach
                    and smoke
                    from new charred campfires.

VI

Orpheus

The Welshman by the pit whose Sabbath voice
Would set the week to peace,
Picked over coal and said he knew
The inside of our god, his transformation
Out of tree, the face in black,
Stamped on the walls he picked. This metaphor,
He said, the pit shaped underneath him into black
And pitied words that moved the leaves or sang
Together flocks, or shook the dull and herded animals.

His pity also took between the rocks
Some still alive who saw the black and second
Hand that clawed them, and he mocked in Welsh
Whatever shades fell back, and cursed and sang
Back to their second death those grave ghosts.

Who found his body and who found his head
And who wiped god off his eyes and face?

Estevan Saskatchewan

A small town bears the mark of Cain,
Or the oldest brother with the dead king's wife
In a foul relation as viewed by sons
Lies on the land, squat, producing
Love's queer offspring only,
Which issue drives the young
To feign a summer madness, consort with skulls,
While the farmer's chorus, a Greek harbinger,
Forecasts by frost or rings about the moon
How ill and black the seeds will grow.

This goodly frame, the earth, each of its sons,
With nature as a text, and common theme
The death of fathers, anguished in betrayal
From the first family returns a sacrifice
Of blood's brother, a splintered eyeball
Groined in the fields, scarecrow to crows.
This warns Ophelia to her morning song,
Bawdy as a lyric in a pretty brain gone bad,
While on those fields the stupid harvest lies.

Ice Palace

Only the blue men
of Saskatchewan
and the blue women
of Quebec

swim these white bone halls
the palace of King Skeleton
and only blue ones could.

Journey through his land alone.
For blue men do not speak
the way you speak, or cry
hail and farewell.

They squeak
like eels on ice

or needles on a gramophone.

Prologue

I think it was burned on. And the smell:
No one would go near it for days after it appeared.
There was hell to pay in the council, everyone
Dredged muck out of the past. The mayor quit.

They tried whitewash. Seen it anyhow, blacker
Than sin on Sunday. Tried burning. Smoke choked
The town for days, the fence was still there.

Bees swarmed, honey of smoke, out of the old
Witch tree and got into the kitchen chimney,
Stung the cook and she quit too.
Slop all over the wall where she threw the pail.
The air was blue with bees and words.

Preacher says,
        Hell fire aint good enough.
Preacher says,
        It burns and it aint burned.
Kind of like drought. The day's coming.
The fine critter bouncing on the hill
Aint the same when she's laid low.
Skinned she's awful.
Like the insides of a calving cow.

And you can't blow the spots off a leopard anyhow.

Epilogue

When our mayor was put out to eat grass
And on the street manholes opened like eyes,
Everyone said it had come from below
Because the street was nervous, empty,
And the sewers rumbled for days, the wires
Sang in the high wind and cracks appeared
In the grey cement like folds in an elephant's hide.

Everyone said it had come from below
Because the banks toppled over like great gods
And fire flamed out of the mouth of the stock exchange,
And our bird-like mayor, a hoofed thing,
Galloped away to the green fields in the country.

Mail Order Catalogue

(logos of things in the outhouse
paradigm of experience
from beginning: abdominal belts
to end: zippers, lightning

the art of communication
icons of the graffitic world):

bound, stretched, boned women
hung by the harps of their hair
the wire of their thighs

unravished brides   fence
an acre of grass, a seed plot

and what mysterious rites
of harrow, plot, and drill

and hired men walking on the hill
all in a blaze of fire, the wire
strung from their hands like harps
fencing the acres

            stays, pants,
the attic urn, scored in the grain
a low relief, a lowing heifer,
a bull on the wall.

Souris Valley

You will ask how I came here. In my 36th year
by libraries and paintings, and the landscape
now northern, a bruised sky, punctured by pines,
and how the university could tolerate me,
what night it was I hung from the rock
and whether my father knew.
                                        I met
murder on the way and the face of a Principal,
in the rock I saw the hands of moralists
and the drowned officer who served my warrant
crying, on my rock this first church.

You will understand how much of this is description,
how in the valley mothers would gather, the river
swollen, the mustard milky and sticky, breasted plant,
and how icy sons blossomed like crystal.

Departure

There was merely a brief note:
"Have seen Edmonton
am leaving at once."
                                I think:
it must have been the buildings
or perhaps the art gallery
or even the university.

But his friends tell me
he had no ambition
his children were slovenly
recently he recovered from a strange disease
he no longer knows what numbers are
nor understands the language spoken here.

Doll on the Mantelpiece

Here on the mantel where a Dresden doll
Looks into a frozen german hill
All is still, chill, white,
Except the red stain on her lips,
The blood of colour there.

She is poised for a dance above the fire,
A hand out for a partner neither here
Nor anywhere. The fire breathes below
A savage noise of wood and she looks out
Over the white hill, still as a doll,
Chill in her world of ivory.

Why do I think of clowns, of emperors,
Of Nietzsche in his tower and all Berlin
Falling in flames while this silly doll
Stands on a fire, calm beside a frozen hill?

Ducks in a Pond

1

Hairy and huge, old sun stood
up to his neck in a slough
and ever from his coronal arm
coins to mallards he threw
and mallards in a spume of mire
leaped to the touch of web and fire.

2

One must have a cold, reedy skin
(touching this question of fire)
to tread out a frothy zeal
under the armpits of a hairy wheel
under the arm of the sweating sun
to maunder in a slough of sweat
and skin, of water touched by fire.

3

About the death of ducks in ice
I know nothing, but mallards know
of Franklin underfoot, his men
on Boothia and their frozen dance
in snowy froth that stoned the eye,
the sun a cataract in a blinding day.

4

The zeal of ducks for noise
(touching this question of fire)
is not the music that I hoped to hear
(Isaiah's coal, the final choir)
but poise of mallards in a pool
as in the pupil of an eye where fire
burned on water seems a pose of praise
sufficient for the gabble of my days.

Notes from the Underground

A woman built herself a cave
    and furnished it with torn machines
    and tree-shaped trunks and dictionaries.
Out of the town where she sprang
    to her cave of rusting texts and springs
    rushed fables of indifferent rape
    and children slain indifferently
    and daily blood.

Would you believe how free I have become
    with lusting after her?
                That I have become
    a melodramatist, my friends ashamed?

I have seen by the light of her burning texts
    how the indifferent blood drips
    from the brass mouths of my friends,
    how at the same table I will eat
    and grow fat.

Her breasts are planets in a reedy slough.
Lie down beside that slough awhile
    and taste the bitter reed

Read in the water how a drowning man
    sings of a free green life.

There Is No One Here Except Us Comedians

1

In what we call dreams I see
a fairground of wheels inside wheels
where I am turned into nobody
nobody's son nobody's daughter

and orphanages
where children
drag toward iron gates yellow dolls
and huge rolling balls
made in the shape of towering fathers

2

I pray nightly for release
I ask of a door shaped like a bat
to fly away with me
I want to be in a wheatfield
stupid as grain yellowing in the sun
I want to be something like a bird,
part reptile, able to stare blankly
for minutes
        at jade trees
        at jewelled grass
        the crystal city

whispering blasphemy
I want to walk over the doors of the city
my bird feet tinkling at keyholes

I want you to know I am innocent
I want you to open the last door
into the field of orphan wheat
the orient grain the green golden corn

Two Part Exercise on a Single Image

I

I come into the desolation
Of this calm September town
Which slants out of morning
Into the wild disaster of sunlight,
And I see that my street is a tree
Split into a thousand sentences
Any one of which can hang me.
The sun shatters my tree
In a wind of light
Into a torch in the unexplained
Interior, luminous with volcanoes,
Dark fig trees, and the white
Question mark of a polar bear.

II

You think it's easy? A matter of words?
You wonder that I'm a poor speller?
Let me tell you this has nothing to do with
Teaching, or even the love of poetry.
It is an eyesore, a stye,
A social disaster. Look for once
At the real, ridiculous self
Crouched in the unexplained interior.
See it looming in the light of
Exploding volcanoes, dark fig trees,
Like the hunched white question mark of
A polar bear.
                    Oh my friend
I too like company
And have ambitions in business.

Song

When the echo of the last footstep dies
and on the empty street you turn your empty eyes,
what do you think you will see?
A hangman and a hanging tree.

When there are no more voices
and yet you hear voices singing
in the hot street,
what do you think will be their song?
Glory to the hangman who is never wrong.

When on the hot sands of your burning mind
iron footsteps clang no more
and blind eyes no longer see
and voices end,
what do you think will be your plea?
Hanging isn't good enough for me.

The Gold Bug

a poisonous bee burst his pod
in the palm of my hand
                          his venom
flowed over my hand like honey

now honoured among men
I gesture with my golden hand
and I speak with the language of money

Palinode

I don't suppose that poems can be made
Of private shame, of shame, or sham
Excesses of the spirit.
                     Modest Locke
Once closed the door to godliness
And in his shaded room saw nothing
Of the wide, bruised sky of spring.
He said, the underbrush is thick,
Until we've hacked a way through it
We cannot know the shape of practical despair.

I say that it was spring,
And it was then as if with prison bars
The ruler sun had strictly lined the air,
As if a kind of Dali plain, empty of bush,
Stretched out, as if the first ants
Of the year crawled on the sky,
And it was then I saw that private men
Were dragging loads of bone and flesh
In sackfuls to the edges of the plain.
I cried to stop it, saying, God, you know,
Inhabits each man's breast. Look at the sky,
The sun is Blake in excess of his glory
Come to clothe the naked twigs, and looked
And saw the drop of blood that hung there
And saw it run and spread and soak the men
And saw it seeping, in the spring, out of those sacks.

The Fire Place

A furnace is of stone and clay,
A fire burns inside the stone,
Beside the flame Fuseli lay,
The heart within it was his own.

Fuseli, when the witch came in,
Raised the roof above his stone,
On her thighs he painted sin,
On her head a horse's mane.

From her lips a vocal moth
Issued screaming to the smoke,
Augustan ladies in their mirth
Gathered folds about her smock.

In the smoking cup a sea,
By the bed a painted ship,
In the door a massive key,
On the floor an open trap.

Coupled with a horse a man
Leans upon her breast; he sighs;
Flaming curtains issue then
In between the witch's thighs.

Pillar of Fire

A man came to my tent door
in the heat of the day, the tent
stretched and slapped in the wind.
All the guy ropes went taut
and I felt my temples stretch
and throb in the noise and heat.

He talked about blowflies,
plague among the swollen cattle.
He asked about the children.
"You are a great nation.
Will you stay here long?"

That night the fire in the tent
vomited a great smoke.
The tent glowed like a furnace.
I dreamt about Egypt and its flies,
a priest dying of cancer.
I am told to breed more children,
try not to think about politics,
remember the Sabbath and my enemies.

Mr Mandel's Sermon

I have heard singing and thought how singing maddens
the singers because their mouths are open in a shriek
and the strained muscles of the faces pull down the eyes
in a clown's cry.
    Around the stake where the dying bear
has lolled for several days the singers are open-mouthed
and at the pit where the bear baited the virgin
         where
the court musicians squeezed the rare mouth-sweat
into the petals of their horns like bees dripping
honey on the horns of lilies
      the song was a bridegroom
pacing his claim to the tent of his blue bride.

This cosmic song was sung my murderous friends
by you who raped the bear's girl before you hurled
her in the pit and you in whom the stake is never still.

Map of Love

I was sure that his children were lousy
and his wife's eczema thickest
around her thighs
    like a map
of a tyrant's gradual conquest
of Europe
    or a medical diagram
of the advanced tumours of love.

Metamorphosis

Looking at her, my eyes magnified by anger,
I saw her nose collapse to nostrils in her face,
her eyes narrow, her eyelids disappear,
her lips extend into a pointed, yellow beak;
I thanked the transformation of my rage
that gave me vision.
                        Later,
I discovered my eyes were little stones
and on my hand instead of hair were quills,
and in my blood, not hers, the reptile crawled.

Intellectual beauty, how we are shrunken now.

The Other Harmony: Not Imitation

Nothing simple: a particular lie
spreads like ink on a Rorschach card
like clouds upon the moon
                              and she
in the inky arms of the octopus
deep in the bottled sea
                              and dizzily
is my squalid, squat, and masculine
mother.

        I made this (decked out
as a dandy) and I have made other
seas
    and shall again in winter
sail farther than Saskatoon or Calgary.

Pictures in an Asylum

The shock is
>   do not honour verity
>   that lie you told, it is here
>   under the sea, under the sea

the shock is
>   do not love so many
>   love is the stone that tears
>   the bladder on the yellow sea

the shock is
>   things are what they seem to be
>   there is no god
>   no love nor verity
>   under the sea

and the shock is
>   sharp as ice-picks in the brain
>   the child is sane
>   the child is sane again

Charles Isaac Mandel

These uplands of the suburban mind,
sunlit, where dwell the lithe ironists,
athletic as greeks, boy-lovers,
mathematical in love as in science.
Formalists. What have I to do with them?
I gather the few relics of my father:
his soiled Tallis, his Tefillin,
the strict black leather of his dark faith.

Landscape

The tree shaped like a lock against the sky
And the river like a door and like a key

The sorrowing sun looks in, there is a rim
Around the world, ships topple from the rim

Into the sun but topple back and still are here,
There is a rim and the river shuts like a door.

The tree shaped like a coffin or a nail
And the river like a dark misshapen door

And the sun crouched in his terrible lair
Looks in on the falling ships, the unmusical

Falling ships, and the trees lined up the wall
Like mourners at my mother's funeral.

Jewish Cemetery in Edmonton

If one could move bloodlessly
through the razor air
                              but
the white blood of the snow
drips on the wounded earth.

Trees, apprehensive as vines,
quiver over the slit veins.

Who, with his mouth, will stop
this cold blood or put his root
or seed into this vain wound?

Day of Atonement: Standing

My Lord, how stands it with me now
Who, standing here before you
(who, fierce as you are, are also just),
Cannot bow down. You order this.
Why, therefore, I must break
If bend I will not, yet bend I must.

But I address myself to you thus,
Covered and alert, and will not bare
My self. Then I must bear you,
Heavy as you are.
                    This is the time
The bare tree bends in the fierce wind
And stripped, my God, springs to the sky.

Overheard at the Gaza Mill

I don't like evasion any more than you do
        but to speak out at this time
        is more dangerous than you might think:
        do you know what they burn on Fridays
        and why, and what they carry back?

Even with an inviolate ethic this happens:
        the market brilliant as blood
        soiled relics on the street
        and the athlete carted, a bundle of bones,
        into the ruined stadium, his owners profiting.

David

all day the gopher-killing boys
    their sling-shot arms
        their gopher-cries

the king insisting
    my poetry must stop

I have written nothing since May

instead
      walk among the boys
gopher-blood on their stretched
hands
      murder will end murder
the saying goes, someone must
do something about the rodents
and poems do not:
            even the doctors
admit that it's plague
ask me about my arms
           look
at my shadow hanging
   like a slingshot

the world turns like a murderous stone
    my forehead aching with stars

Songs from the Book of Samuel

i

the intellect does not age, the body dies
daily the mind declares its lies
about the soul, about the self
about the body and its ageless cries

now mind grows freer as the body dies
daily the body ages in its lies
about the mind, about the self
about the mind's clear sense of paradise

ii

I forgive the adulterer, I forgive the song
I forgive the straw man in my bed
I forgive the old man his lies about the bed
I forgive my armies for their arms
I forgive the generals for their boots
and the mayors for their homes
and the councillors
                 my mother
for her prophecies, my father
for his mistaken comfort in failure
my teachers for their religion
I forgive the girl's face in the flower
the instrumental poet hung on his strings
the colonies for the times they did not eat
I forgive the food of the armies
and the carpets under the general's feet
I forgive the poet for lying about god
I forgive god for tomorrow
I forgive the arisen prophet
the man who is a weapon
the weapon
death
the song
the singer dying in his song
even myself

Cold Pastoral

I thought someone said cathedral
    stature of gold
     emperor's bird
and eyes through shining hair.

I thought someone said drowning
    gather of weed
     swirling word
and shining eyes through water.

No one ever said ice
    blood
    wind
or eyes in the cadaver

Thief Hanging in Baptist Halls

After a Sculpture by George Wallace

Amid the congratulations of summer,
polite vegetation, deans, a presbyterian sun,
brick minds quaintly shaped in gothic and glass,
here where the poise and thrust of speech
gleams like polished teak
I did not expect to see myself.

But there he hangs
shrugging on his hung lines,
soft as a pulped fruit or bird
in his welded soft suit of steel.

I wish he would not shrug
and smile weakly at me
as if ashamed that he is hanging there,
his dean's suit fallen off, his leg cocked
as if to run
or (too weak, too tired, too undone)
to do what can be done
about his nakedness.

Why should he hang there,
my deanship, my insulting self, all undone?

Carleton University: January 1961

To George Johnston

Imagine a speaking rock: stone-dumb
mountains lean over Ottawa
but even the dumb stone spires
of Parliament Hill aspire to speech.

There is something raucous in Ottawa;
the P.M.'s speech is coarse,
brash the Privy Council's course
between Hull and the unspeakable Laurentians.

I think of a child's yell of pain
when he is speared by malicious tables,
explanation animate, mythical, fabulous,
and then of you, articulate climber,
bruised by stony syntax
on the mountains of Gawain's English.

How many beastly tables have you slain
where Carleton and its new cement
utter a few blue nouns and glassy verbs
between the howling trains and muzzled snow?

On Yonge Street

After Raymond Souster

seeing your head weave
        your cheeks twitch
        your shoulders jump
I wonder who hit you
        who do you hate

and who will you take on next
        at forty, the punch
        hard as before, reflexes
        quick, your eyes clear

don't you know they will get you
        in the ring or in some alley
        that they will break your mouth
that even the best go blind
        hear unevident birds

or do you care, dreaming of brutes
        buckled and crushed
        the great roar
and the white centre blind with light?

The Comedians

You might have expected music
But they move so slowly they make no sound.
Like swimmers they put their large hands
Up before their huge red mouths
As if to shove mountains of water
Inches over so they can breathe.

And yet you think you hear gasps,
Snuffling, muffled yelps, occasional
Screams when one wallops the other
Or with a paddle shuffles on his enormous feet
Toward his kneeling unsuspecting friend.

Sometimes in their drowning motions
They remove their arms and heads
And walk in their bodies like barrels.

No longer do I care for those critics
Who plead with me that Whitman is God.
As for that other poet, he was lying too.
Warmed by outlandish currents
I have begun to build an aquarium
Tolerant only for tropical fish
Who move like swimmers without sound
And nuzzle one another with their golden mouths.

Secret Flower

Sometimes you are a house
sometimes you unfold
ages and ages old
    you are sometimes
    a house with four rooms
    and four kings
    and four queens
secret flower
of my own design.

Deeper and more secret
darker and older
you unfold.

I have watched lovers
drop from your petals
into the room of kings
before the table of judges.

How can this be? It is Sunday.
My children are making paper men
no one has been poisoned
no one has been hung
there is even laughter in the room.

Darker and still more secret
older and unfolded
beyond my designing heart
beyond even my crying out
through your four rooms
past the hanging tree
beyond the swaying lovers
beyond the judges

who is that lying on the green carpet?
who is being carried on the stone tablet?
why do these gesture and posture before me?

I kneel before the four-armed god
gather up the shredded paper heads
and turn toward the suddenly open door.

The Damp Pilgrim

Was it the mouth?
The air around that castle stank of moat.
Westward a few pilgrims dragged along
Up to the steepled hill now steeped in sun
The growing shadows of their pointed hoods.
And damp inside, damp hung in mist,
Damp hung in ropes of froth along the walls.
I say the brilliant castle stank of moat.

It was in Holland or in Hungary.
The King collected all his furs, and still
He shivered, shook, and cursed the damp.
The Queen wept for her gems.
The pilgrims moved toward the steepled peak.

Clang! went the jester in the court.
He shook his mitred locks and rang
As hollow as a bell hung in a well.
Clang answered from the chains that hung below.

I would leave the court, leave hall, leave
Hollow echoing and damp and find some room
Gone yellow, dry, and dusty with old time
As parched and faded as the pages of my book.

Hippolytus

Lately I have been dreaming of horses

I have known mothers larger than boxcars
carrying the freight of years and wars
toward some stockyard of their minds
where they can count the slaughtered time

I too know something of punishment
there have been drownings even here
beside the dry reeds of the lakeless fields
hands have been held out to me
I dare not touch beside that unseen water
and once a beaten animal stumbled by
looking like someone's brother

easier then to praise
the strong in one another's arms
testing the machinery of love
the freight that moves the world's
horizons
            everyone knows the rules
what to ignore, when and how to whip
the beaten and to bruise the animals

at the edge of these dark waters
hearing the drums of the world movers
again begins the sound of hoofs
I see the wet heaving horses of a last rain

House of Candy

Larches charred still leaning in the swamp,
I stumble here. What do I know of muskeg?
Woodsmen I have met in stories saved young girls.
It was the smoking hearts of casual rodents
They threw before the queen, her clouded eyes.

If I go forward to the blackened tower,
What must I learn about this offering?
How in my bloodless hands will I take blood
Or how appease the queen, her unencumbered arms?

Hunters darkened stare through sullen smoke
As if to see my shape where larches stand
Or find me in the smouldering stump of pine
Or like some candied house, a crystal rock,
Or marvellous and abstract in a cave,
All bearded whisper and prophetic eye.

They do not know how at the story's end,
Duller than prose, I turned toward the south,
Sought out the urgent maiden, warned her of the queen,
Then drove my knife into her heart to save a passing rat.

A Cage of Oats

To James Reaney and Jay Macpherson

How many prisons do I count?
Here is the wall I first ran from
and here there is a second wall,
the wall I ran against to flee
the first, and here there is a cage.

Inside the cage there is a second cage.
Inside the second cage there is a third.

Inside the third
there is a bird.

A Quaker holds a box of oats
on which a Quaker holds a box.
A mirror mirrors oats
for oats are mirrors of their crops
which farmer-quaker-man will thresh
and eat to put the seeds inside
the Quaker man who holds a box.

There may be stars inside of stones
(or other stones): inside of stars
there may be burning seeds.

What boxed bird so great
it can eat
stone, man, star and seed?

Cassandra

This has nothing to do with brothels.

Sometimes it seems my daughter or my wife
or my neighbour's wife, bright-eyed,
imitates an image out of sleep. They walk
as if I had dwindled, looking past me
toward unreasonable parliaments
crouching beside senatorial hills.

I have been practising this poetry in secret.
Also I have made advances toward pregnant women.
But there have been no unusual shadows,
all the swimming pools remain clear of blood,
and by the gates the watcher has not raised his arms.

To My Children

A rose grew in my head
My father lay dead
My mother fell among stones
Two flowers grew in my loins

I sing to my blossoming wife
My father is dead
My mother abandoned her life
Why should I lay down my head

Stony and brittle my days
My children sing psalms
The rabbis are ancient and wise
Blessed be my flowering names

Nude

I apologize to my children
for unplayed games, the Arthurs
I wasn't in the child's nighthood
poetry is a demanding art

sometimes I think I am a city
there is a steel furnace in my heart
trains rush up and down my arms
toward terminals where lovers meet
on the tips of my fingers
my head is a builder's project
full of unsold homes
                          around my thighs
a garden of Boschian animals
carrying bedpans
                    somewhere
(inside) loinward? Pancreatic?
Glandular as in brain or neck?
Anywhere there inside
watery and dismal
                        a tremulous
fish and something utterly nude.

The Meaning of the I Ching

i

unopened
        book of old men
        orange-blossom book
                before me
you were
        how could you contain me?

do you not see I am the mouths
of telegraphs and cemeteries?
my mother groaned like the whole
of Western Union to deliver
my message
        and yelling birthdays
that unrolled from my lungs
like ticker-tape for presidents
about to be murdered
          I sped
on a line that flew
to the vanishing point of the west

before I was
        you were
unopened book
        do not craze me
with the odour of orange-blossom

do not sit there
like smiling old men

        how could you contain me?

ii

under my fingers words form themselves
it's crazy to talk of temples in this day
but light brightens on my page
like today moving against the wooden house
all shapes change and yet stay
as if they were marble in autumn
as if in the marbled yellow autumn
each western house becomes a shrine
stiff against the age of days
under my fingers stiffly formed

I will walk in streets that vanish
noting peculiar elms like old women
who will crash under the storm of sun
that breaks elm, woman, man
into a crumble of stump and bark
until the air is once more clear
in the sane emptiness of fall

iii

my body speaks to me
as my arms say: two are one
as my feet say: earth upon earth
as my knees say: bow down, unhinge yourself
as my cells say: we repeat the unrepeatable

the book speaks: arrange yourself in the form
                    that will arrange you

before I was: colours that hurt me
                    arranged themselves in me

before I was: horizons that blind me
                    arranged themselves in me

before I was: the dead who speak to me
                    arranged themselves in me

iv

I am the mouths
of smiling old men

there rises from me
the scent of orange-blossoms

I speak in the words
of the ancient dead

arranged
in the raging sun
in the stiffening age of days

and in the temple of my house

The Milk of Paradise

1

Marvel upon marvel the berries of the sun
inflame the tumbling waters of my limbs
I am given to such visions: wide-eyed
luminous men walk through a hairy land
toward a milky glade where goats bleat

2

I put away this last unfinished poem
to think with trouble of a friend
who wrote me and whose words I scorned

Streetlights

they're not sunflowers
yet they burn on their stems
like the golden eyes of those other plants

and they bend
in such an iron complaint
toward the street's inverted sky

I'd like to think
they know as much of final things
as any living creature who endures the dark.

Woodbine

When a crooked man meets beauty
You think there'd be shouting in the streets

Believe me, I have gone about with pails on my head
so that my friends would recognize me

I wish there were no allegories
I wish the doctors could do something about my forked tongue

Lord, Lord, pollution everywhere
But I breathe still
                    and breathless, sweet
woodbine, colour of honey, touches my skin
as if my unbelieving eyes made no difference at all

Signatures

In the eyes of lovers and mothers
gardens recently frighten me, grunts
from earth, deep growing things.
I think of Schweitzer dead at last,
his organs mutilated by those roots.
As for the tumult in the streets,
there are knives in water, in taps,
and once I took up from the tracks
beside the water-tower in my town
a huge beet, hairy and huge, that lay
in my hands like an under-water thing.

Thugs rampage. Marines draw down the head,
ancient and tight, her hair in ecstasy,
some Viet-Nam woman who had loved deeply
or who'd wept over her gunman son,
draw down into a pool that head
I've seen in paintings where there was no blood.

The room is alien: threats uttered
where only the print and I engage
our locked dialogue.
                        Out of the blind
years, remotely, as in earth stirred
by slugs or worms, heaves a memory
of beets and roots; things unuttered
and unutterable, echoing out of print,
out of streams, a signature of rage.

Girl on a High Wire

Do you think I'd sit here staring
if I knew how to work a chair-lift
or lacked this odd taste for vertigo?

What if I dare you to jump, saying, ah
my hurt bird, I will catch you—
and if I weren't there (someone calling,
my son pointing at camels or wanting
to pee) when your eyes became horizons?
Or if you fell
into the well of bankers, mid-wives,
my brother-in-law, the Prudential Life
Insurance Company?
                    I see them,
heroine, hefting you, their applause
ringing your head with the clatter of zircons,
mouths blowing little balloons of praise.

The great globe circles.
Soldiers fall into muddy rivers.
Boys walk the tightrope of their prison yard.

I can no longer look at telephone wires,
the vanishing point of your unfinished portrait.

I shall devote myself to entomology,
practise weight-lifting with dinky toys,
but who will keep me from my crooked prayers,
those mad doves that fling haloes around you?

Houdini

I suspect he knew that trunks are metaphors,
could distinguish between the finest rhythms
unrolled on rope or singing in a chain
and knew the metrics of the deepest pools

I think of him listening to the words
spoken by manacles, cells, handcuffs,
chests, hampers, roll-top desks, vaults,
especially the deep words spoken by coffins

escape, escape: quaint Harry in his suit
his chains, his desk, attached to all attachments
how he'd sweat in that precise struggle
with those binding words, wrapped around him
like that mannered style, his formal suit

and spoken when? by whom? What thing first said
"there's no way out?"; so that he'd free himself,
leap, squirm, no matter how, to chain himself again,
once more jump out of the deep alive
with all his chains singing around his feet
like the bound crowds who sigh, who sigh.

The Speaking Earth

grandfathers fall into it
their mighty beards muffled in grass

and admirals, the sea-sounding men

lovers fall into the earth
like rain on wet dark bodies

listen, our lady earth flowers
into the sea-green language
of grass and drowned admirals

listen: in bearded branches
clasped like broken hands
admiring birds
lovers singing of their kiss
before and after all the words

Listen, the Sea

yes what is
I'm learning

by your leave
leaving
      rising
to leave
      return
and turn
        we
deliberate
by the waves
rhythm casual
move
     tidal

as
   traffic

as
   the sea-women

neither are they
certain uncertain
but with us

within
     their song
here and
      hear
it is

Meditation on the Papyrus of Ani

sparrows discovering my eyes
leave me undisciplined

a trouble to my family

my soul, my indolent soul
why have you not learned the 66 names of god?

The Waggoner's Song

I've learned
            not to believe
in those hairy monks with their burning trees

            but that story
about the slain daughter
where we wept in one another's arms
that was good
            now I know
something more about agony
                        I know
perfection is a poem I never wrote

one about children
a tree
a curious bird
            well, there are other songs

The Madness of Our Polity

I saw this. On the prairies where I lived
a boy who put a needle in a gopher's eye
knew more of civil law than all my friends.

What other emblem do you need?

Poem

Lately, the Chinese paintings on my wall
utter profanities
                    and yet, no Western man
has set his foot upon those hills
or muddied with his hands that silent waterfall.

The President and the Chairman Meet

when great men greet each other
with tea and wine and ceremony
small ones draw close
to guard themselves

On the Death of Ho Chi Minh

toward the end
he became frail as rice paper
his beard whispering thin ideograms

how unlike the great carved storm
that was Marx's face
                              how unlike
the darkness and fury
in Beethoven's head
                              scarcely
anything to be consumed

bombs destroy   destroy
but cannot touch his body now
or burn his poems

In the Fifty-seventh Century of Our Lord

semitic and secret I plan new evasions,
survival, the tribal rite
                              to be
horribly chummy with god
as if he cared
                    in particular
about my politics
my plans for adultery
my marvellous scheme to blame it
on my neighbour's blameless wife

From the North Saskatchewan

when on the high bluff discovering
the river cuts below
                send messages
we have spoken to those on the boats

I am obsessed by the berries they eat
all night odour of Saskatoon
and an unidentifiable odour
something baking
              the sun
never reaches the lower bank

I cannot read the tree markings

today the sky is torn by wind:
a field after a long battle
strewn with corpses of cloud

give blessings to my children
speak for us to those who sent us here
say we did all that could be done
we have not learned
what lies north of the river
or past those hills that look like beasts

Letter to Be Opened Later

Tell them I did not vote Liberal
though I have taken bribes.
I want them to know that secretly
I admired the old red flag.

If they ask about our gods
explain I did pray to the angels
by all their right names:
                              Mr. President
Your Worship, Dear Sir, Your Honour.

Listen:

I've told my analyst everything
except the bit about the girl student.

I don't know why the inspector threatens me
with letters rimmed in red.

Neither Here nor There

somewhere, I'm told, in fields darker than sleep
browse dreaming beasts with unhurt eyes
while walnut-coloured men in wind-swept voices
revolve their prayers as if they were wheels or stars

it isn't that way: one by one my poems fall apart
like a cooked onion
                          in the next house
a window opens once
                              you wouldn't believe
what my blonde neighbour said
                                        anyhow
next year the carnival will be bigger
they say they've got a real live junkie in a rage

The Anarchist-Poets

Step carefully through this rubble of words.
Can you really say which wrecks were once poems,
which weapons?
         who once ran havoc
through these cities of language
scattering flowers of darkness,
black bursts of unmeaning?
        what guerrillas
frantic for peace, love, home, nation,
government, even for death itself?

The Apology

I take back my apology:
       the table the hassock were not moved
       the radio opens its great ears
       to assassinations, weathers, sinkings
       but its four white eyes do not blink
       its clock goes round
       I want to connect with the radio
       I want to put its plugs in my ears
       and hear my throat announce that even
       the Leafs are winning
       I want the table to appreciate my
       delight in its leaves: I will stand on
       four legs and try hard to be wooden and
       brown with folding leaves
       I will fold and unfold my leaves
         like a wooden butterfly
       and birthday cards can be put on me
       I will support birthday cards and letters
        demanding rooms in hotels/   and typewriters
       connecting tables and stars
I will love the light olive of the Olivetti
if necessary I will drink olive oil
I have no objection to becoming an olive myself
even in a martini

even a bugged martini
                    but though before my spread hands
                    though before the blessings and welcomes
                    in the fake Hebrew gestures I make to
                    the world
                    though my agony neither burns nor moves
                    tables and radios/ and my love does nothing
                    oh nothing to change them
I'm not going to apologize
I take back all the sorry clowns I tried to give you
(I will give them to you again, being a dream of Chaplin and
the short-haired girls who flicker in his hunch-backed gaze)
because you are not the table or radio
because you are not the idea of an olive or an olive
or an olive's idea of itself
because I can be tables but not you
and all the words fall hopelessly at your feet
like the bad idea of a plastic bouquet in hot weather
or the new kinds of toys which never quite fit in their parts
or that Zeppelin *Mad* magazine once tried to make me make
and it couldn't not only not fly it couldn't be put together
to fly though I managed the first three parts of a Voop
which is a great mouth and one foot and things hanging around
the mouth and foot
                    let me work hard at becoming tables or radios
                    I will be precise and they will continue
                    as if I weren't there at all

Psalm 24

What did you expect?
You, who drove me to mad alphabets
and taught me all the wrong words.

Isn't it enough that I've failed?

It's your scripture. You read it.

Hebraism

The law is the law and is
terribly Hebrew which is as you
know mostly poems about cooking
and meat to be cured in water and
salt and children to be counted
for pages of generation amid clean
and also unclean women

Pictures in an Institution

1

Notice: all mirrors will be covered
the mailman is forbidden to speak
professors are confined to their offices
faculties no longer exist.

2

I speak of what I know,
how uncle Asher, spittle on his lips,
first typed with harvest hands the fox
across a fence and showing all good men
come to their country's aid rushed off to Israel
there to brutalize his wife and son

how step-grandfather Barak wiped
sour curds out of his curly beard
before he roared the Sabbath in my ears
what Sara, long his widow, dreamed
the night she cried: God, let him die at last,
thinking perhaps of Josef who had lost
jewels in Russia where the Cossack rode
but coughed his stomach out in Winnipeg

Your boredom does not matter. I take,
brutal to my thoughts, these lives, defy
your taste in metaphor; the wind-break
on the farm that Barak plowed to dust
makes images would ruin public poetry.

The rites of love I knew:
how father cheated brother, uncle, son,
and bankrupt-grocer, that we might eat
wrote doggerel verse, later took his wife,
my mother, in the English way beside my bed.
Why would he put his Jewishness aside?
Because there was no bread?

                                    Or out of spite
that doctors sliced his double rupture,
fingered spleen, and healed his bowel's ache?

Lovers lie down in glades, are glad.
These, now in graves, their headstones sunk,
knew nothing of such marvels, only God, his ways,
owning no texts of Greek or anthropology.

                        3

Notice: the library is closed to all who read
                 any student carrying a gun
                 registers first, exempt from fines,
                 is given thirteen books per month,
                 one course in science, one in math,
                 two options
                                  campus police
                 will see to co-eds' underwear

                        4

These names I rehearse:
                        Eva, Isaac,
Charley, Yetta, Max
                  now dead
or dying or beyond my lies

till I reeling with messages
and sick to hold again their bitter lives
put them, with shame, into my poetry.

                        5

Notice: there will be no further communication
                 lectures are cancelled
                 all students are expelled
                 the reading of poetry is declared a public crime

News Item

man throws himself onto
Ottawa's eternal flame

suffers

superficial burns

(Toronto Star, Oct. 23, 1970)

First Political Speech

first, in the first place, to begin with, secondly,
in the second place, lastly

again, also, in the next place, once more, moreover,
furthermore, likewise, besides, similarly, for example,
for instance, another

then, nevertheless, still, however, at the same time,
yet, in spite of that, on the other hand, on the contrary

certainly, surely, doubtless, indeed, perhaps, possibly,
probably, anyway, in all probability, in all likelihood,
at all events, in any case

therefore, consequently, accordingly, thus, as a result,
in consequence of this, as might be expected

the foregoing, the preceding, as previously mentioned

as already stated

Transition Table
from *Learning to Write* by Ernest H. Winter (Second
Revised Edition) Macmillan (Toronto, 1961), p.156.

Manner of Suicide

hanging themselves
taking poison in the top of high trees
throwing themselves on swiftly revolving circular saws
exploding dynamite in their mouths
thrusting red hot pokers down their throats
hugging red hot stoves
freezing to death on piles of ice
in refrigerator cars
lacerating their throats on barbed wire fences
drowning themselves head downwards in barrels
suffocating themselves head downwards in chimneys
diving into white-hot coke ovens
throwing themselves into craters of volcanoes
shooting themselves with ingenious combinations of
a rifle and a sewing machine
strangling themselves with their hair
swallowing poisonous spiders
piercing their hearts with corkscrews and
darning needles
cutting their throats with handsaws and sheepshears
hanging themselves with grape vines
swallowing strips of underclothing and buckles
of suspenders
forcing teams of horses to tear their heads off
drowning themselves in vats of soft soap
plunging into retorts of molten glass
jumping into slaughter-house tanks of blood
decapitation with homemade guillotines
self-crucifixion

Man Against Himself, Karl Menninger, *passim.*

Narrative Poem

the point is
the story
       that
one no one
        told

and yet
      cattle
on lean flanked
land leaning
toward plain

and yet
      shacks
coal fire
despair
     the
barbed wire
wolf willow
river rice

but never
a third act
plotting

end or
even

beginning

land
and long
land
   and
land

Praise

even the smallest room
defines
       how we might be
without enclosing space

I praise
       private
secret touching

Estevan, 1934

remembering the family we
called breeds   the Roques
their house smelling of urine
my mother's prayers before
the dried fish she cursed
them for their dirtiness their
women I remember too
                 how
seldom they spoke and
they touched one another

even when the sun killed
cattle and rabbis
          even
in the poisoned slow air
like hunters
       like lizards
they touched   stone
they touched
          earth

Edmonton, 1967

as if by Colville
I mean "hard edge"
stucco   white wall
gravel &
          legs
in one direction shadows
leaning & midget
above the pavement narrows
rapid as the river
                    everything
disappears
          neatness: axiomatic
          houses   here
now gone
          "You are impatient
with poetry" my friend writes
from Iceland

Oil Refineries: Edmonton

squat
     (are)   .
and there
          fraction-
ary silver re-
flections   flat
distillation
(silver) in
flat
eye
     pulled side-
ways a slit in
the mind (&) all

a line   against   some
poem
          not   there

At Wabamun the Calgary Power Station

leans white in the moon
light puts white slabs up
light shanty whiteness leans

as if it owned the land

daytime horses crop grass
unknowing transformers hum

transformers   at the word
it takes on fiery hair
blazing it transmits
messages furious and hairy
it sends and receives from stars
ancient planets   people
who speak like horses new words

then sparks perform dead
parabolas and loops die
fireplace quietens it is
morning it is light only
the power the power hums

and the lake grows green
again in sunlight
                    it is
morning algae and weeds
thicken
          the green lake
wobbles
          we look at
each other   alien forms

From "Wabamun"

1

lake
    holds
            sun   moon   stars

      trees
          hold

stars   moon   sun

2

only
    waves   motion
    sun   dancing

no sun

only
      light
hurting
in its
      endless
dance

3

on water
many suns
       here there
fires   then
silent comedians
perch jumping

gulls

4

each day I
step
     farther
into dark water

once I will
know
        no longer
whether
        that one
floating
        is myself
or the light
            one
standing
        on the red
pier

5

to have come to this

simplicity

        to know

only

    the absolute

calm
    lake

    before

    night

DREAMING
BACKWARDS

It is from the *Dreaming Back* of the dead, though not from that of persons associated with our past, that we get the imagery of ordinary sleep. Much of the dream's confusion comes from the fact that the image belongs to some unknown person.... "We have no power," said an inhabitant [of the spirit state], "except to purify our intention," and when I asked of what, replied: "Of complexity."

W. B. Yeats, *A Vision*

from *Trio*

Minotaur Poems

I

It has been hours in these rooms,
the opening to which, door or sash,
I have lost. I have gone from room to room
asking the janitors who were sweeping up
the brains that lay on the floors,
the bones shining in the wastebaskets,
and once I asked a suit of clothes
that collapsed at my breath and bundled
and crawled on the floor like a coward.
Finally, after several stories,
in the staired and eyed hall,
I came upon a man with the face of a bull.

II

My father was always out in the garage
building a shining wing, a wing
that curved and flew along the edge of blue air
in that streamed and sunlit room
that smelled of oil and engines
and crankcase grease, and especially
the lemon smell of polish and cedar.
Outside there were sharp rocks, and trees,
cold air where birds fell like rocks
and screams, hawks, kites, and cranes.
The air was filled with a buzzing and flying
and the invisible hum of a bee's wings was honey
in my father's framed and engined mind.
Last Saturday we saw him at the horizon
screaming like a hawk as he fell into the sun.

III

They chose among us in the fall of the year,
by lot, behind fierce masks designed of sign
to ward off the imminent descent of the sun people;
someone talked of a dying god, as if
the young ones among us believed in that
any more, others cautioned us against the voices
we were always supposed to hear and these
were stubborn about the women crying.
I remembered the face of the one who brought me here
when they drew my name in the hall,
it was her persuasions in the beginning,
something about fathers.
                        Like the others, before this
I saw only their breasts that appeared on the walls,
legs moving in unison, the swaying of sweat-stained
bodies and their half closed eyes:
all the talk about signs when I knew
the boys were only waiting for the time
when the women undressed, as they always did,
                        snickering
in those same fields that make a dawn in vision
where birds begin to live in rocks and screams.
It is hard to feel free of accusation
because of eyes
although there is a difference between revelation
and action bellied into life, between
believing in voices
and knowing the chances that we have to take.

IV

Now I am dressed in a multitude of rooms
like a Chinese box, and slip from covers
into covers   Dawn will not help me nor
the day's exposure   I am a prodigious pun
to hide and show myself between these walls
this otherwise where sunlight
dressed in a tweed suit pursues me
or a stranger in the rooms
        and footfalls on the stairs
and eyes   and over all
    the whispering and chattering of the walls
        the pipes and hammered arteries of the place.

Is that a revelation in a field of light
competing with a shadow on the rock?
A bird's shadow seen from here?
Or a cloud between the sky and land
footed and patterned into phrases?

It is hours since I have been in here.
If I had once seen anything
except birds,
rocks, land, and all winter long
                the ice and snow.

V

Within these walls I am to look for light
Or hold an abstract in my hand as firm
As apples or the golden bar the older men
Returned to us. Remember that. That spring
There were those crowds and crowds below the cliffs
This side of town and all along the beach,
Flags out, booths filled with toys, and one,
The better salesman of the lot, a beggar
From the north had miniatures of bars
That went like hotcakes. Fleece for the crowd.
A replica to keep you as it kept our men
This winter past. Then noise, flocks wheeling overhead,
The painted ship, a bauble on the sea, came like a toy
To harbour.

       And the tall bronzed men descended
Between the cheers and speeches at the harbour mouth,
Talk about campaigns in lands we'd never heard of,
Cheers and lewd remarks and laughter, the look
In other eyes, and counting of the crew
And stooping at the gaps aghast.
That was another death, the shock in surf,
The rock's point of view, the hawk
Momentarily composing before the fall
His target of a landscape from the sky.
The trailing plume before the dark.
Night on the beach and smoke
            from the new charred campfires.

VI

Orpheus

The Welshman by the pit whose Sabbath voice
Would set the week to peace, or end a day,
Picked over coal and said he knew within
The inside of our god, his transformation
Out of tree, the face in black, faced out of coal,
Stamped on the walls he picked his useful metaphor,
He said, the pit shaped underneath him in black
And pitied words that moved the leaves or sang
Together flocks, or shook the dull and herded animals.
His pity also took between the rocks
Some still alive who saw the black and second
Hand that clawed them, and he mocked in Welsh
Whatever shades fell back, and cursed and sang
Back to their second death those grave ghosts.

Who found his body and who found his head
And who wiped god from off his eyes and face?

Estevan Saskatchewan

A small town bears the mark of Cain,
Or the oldest brother with the dead king's wife
In a foul relation as viewed by sons,
Lies on the land, squat, producing
Love's queer offspring only,
Which issue drives the young
To feign a summer madness, consort with skulls,
While the farmer's chorus, a Greek harbinger,
Forecasts by frost or rings about the moon
How ill and black the seeds will grow.

This goodly frame, the earth, each of its sons,
With nature as a text, and common theme
The death of fathers, anguished in betrayal
From the first family returns a sacrifice
Of blood's brother, a splintered eyeball
Groined in the fields, scarecrow to crows.
This warns Ophelia to her morning song,
Bawdy as a lyric in a pretty brain gone bad,
While on those fields the stupid harvest lies.

from *Fuseli Poems*

Notes from the Underground

A woman built herself a cave
    and furnished it with torn machines
    and tree-shaped trunks and dictionaries.
Out of the town where she sprang
    to her cave of rusting texts and springs
    rushed fables of indifferent rape
    and children slain indifferently
    and daily blood.

Would you believe how free I have become
    with lusting after her?
                That I have become
    a melodramatist, my friends ashamed?

I have seen by the light of her burning texts
    how the indifferent blood drips
    from the brass mouths of my friends,
    how at the same table I have supped
    and grown fat.

Her breasts are planets in a reedy slough.
Lie down beside that slough awhile
    and taste the bitter reeds.

Read in the water how a drowning man
    sings of a free green life.

Ducks in a Pond

1

Hairy and huge, old sun stood
up to his neck in a slough
and ever from his coronal arm
coins to mallards he threw
and mallards in a spume of mire
leaped to the touch of web and fire.

2

One must have a cold, reedy skin
(touching this question of fire)
to tread out a froth of zeal
under the armpits of the hairy wheel
under the arm of the sweating sun
to maunder in a slough of sweat
a skin of water touched by fire.

3

About the death of ducks in ice
I know nothing, but mallards know
of Franklin underfoot, his men
on Boothia and their frozen dance
in snowy froth that stoned the eye,
the sun a cataract in a blinding day.

4

The zeal of ducks for noise
(touching this question of fire)
is not the music that I hoped to hear
(Isaiah's coal, the final choir)
but poise of mallards in a pool
as in the pupil of an eye where fire
burned on water seems a pose of praise
sufficient for the gabble of my days.

Palisade of Images

Stevens being dead: 75 - 3/8/55
I owe him this
                "just one more truth, one more
Element in the immense disorder of truths."
                                        not pastoral
                                        nothing for Dylan
                                        done in early
that great hospital gong silent and the tongue
a useless clapper in the bell
but for a better arrangement
a kind of insurance against doubt

arranging bees honeycomb feeling
into wax
into box
and sweetness crumbles on the tongue
to merely crystal, the calligraphy of taste

or the iconographic fly, perpetual puritan,
                        imagines on carcasses
                        clean blue colonies
and at the shudder of my step
dissolves society, is stinking fly

well, Wallace has his clean eternal order now
clatter of card-sorting in his office for his poem
stamps him
flips him
into a strong box, honeycomb of unlettered cards

perhaps the Great Bear feeds on such papery dew
his paw inside the blighted log of Time
perhaps ants and flies from all the centuries
run out of it over his hairy chest
I write this in hot August, my room
palisaded with images
                of bees
                of flies
of cardboard Stevens in his honeycomb of lies.

Two Part Exercise on a Single Image

I

I come into the desolation
Of this calm September town
Which slants out of morning
Into the wild disaster of sunlight,
And I see that my street is a tree
Split into a thousand sentences
Any one of which can hang me.
Birds in that tree utter phrases
Which are pebbles of glass that flow
Into the light of a river,
And the paned mirror of the river
Gives up the restless image
Of a man walking down slanting streets
Like corridors in "Blood of a Poet."
The sun shatters my tree
In a wind of light
Into a torch in the unexplained
Interior, luminous with volcanoes,
Dark fig trees, and the white
Hunched question mark of a polar bear.

II

You think it is easy? A matter of words?
And wonder that I'm a poor speller?
Let me tell you this has nothing to do
With teaching or even the love of poetry.
It is the calamity of an eyesore, a stye,
A social disaster. Look for once
At the real, ridiculous humped self
Crouched in the unexplained interior.
See it looming in the light
Of exploding volcanoes and dark fig trees
Like the hunched white question mark
Of a polar bear.
Oh my friend, I too like company
And have ambitions in business.

Acis

There was her message. Suddenly
His blood had turned to water.
She looked into his eyes and saw
They swam, no shore behind them,
Looking toward the green and lighted sea,
A fish-like stare, a dolphin memory.

City Park Merry-Go-Round

Freedom is seldom what you now believe.
Mostly you circle round and round the park:
Night follows day, these horses never leave.

Like children, love whatever you conceive,
See then our world as lights whirled in the dark.
Freedom is seldom what you now believe.

Your world moves up and down or seems to weave
And still you pass you pass the same ringed mark.
Night follows day, these horses never leave.

You thought your past was here, you might retrieve
That wild illusion whirling in the dark.
Freedom is seldom what you now believe.

Sick on that circle you begin to grieve.
You wish the ride would end you could escape the park.
Night follows day, these horses never leave.

Mostly you circle round and round the park.
You'd give your life now to be free to leave.
Freedom is seldom what you now believe.
Night follows day, theses horses never leave.

Pillar of Fire

A man came to my tent door
in the heat of the day, the tent
stretched and slapped in the wind.
All the guy ropes went taut
And I felt my temples stretch
and throb in the noise and heat.

He talked about blowflies,
plague among the swollen cattle.
He asked about the children.
"You are a great nation.
Will you stay here long?"

That night the fire in the tent
vomited a great smoke.
The tent glowed like a furnace.
I dreamt about Egypt and its flies,
a priest dying of cancer.
I am told to breed more children,
try not to think about politics,
remember the Sabbath and my enemies.

Palinode

I don't suppose that poems can be made
Of private shame, or shame, or sham
Excesses of the spirit. Modest Locke
Once closed the door to godliness
And in his shaded room saw nothing
Of the wide, bruised sky of spring
Wrapped in its bandages of cloud,
And said, the underbrush is thick,
Until we've hacked a way through it
We cannot know the shape of huge,
Deformed and practical Despair
Prowling in the woods beside his lair
Heaped with the bones of gay adventurers.

I say that it was spring, and it was then
As if with prison bars the ruler sun
Had strictly lined the air, as if
A kind of Dali plain, empty of bush,
Stretched out, as if the first ants
Of the year crawled on the wound
That lipped the iodine-stained sky,
And it was then I saw that private men
Were dragging loads of bone and flesh
In sackfuls to the edges of the plain.
I cried to stop it, saying, God, you know,
Inhabits each man's breast. Look at the sky,
The sun is Blake in excess of his glory
Come to clothe the naked twigs, and looked
And saw the drop of blood that hangs there
And saw it run and spread and soak the men
And saw it seeping, in the spring, out of those sacks.

Prologue

I think it was burned on. And the smell.
No one would go near it for days after it appeared.
There was hell to pay in the council, everyone
Dredged muck out of the past. The mayor quit.

They tried whitewash. See it anyhow, blacker
Than sin on Sunday. Tried burning. Smoke choked
The town for days, and the fence was still there.

Bees swarmed, honey of smoke, out of the old
Witch tree and got into the kitchen chimney,
Stung the cook and she quit too.
Slop all over the wall where she threw the pail.
The air was blue with bees and words.

Preacher says,
        Hell fire aint good enough.
Preacher says,
        It burns and it aint burned.
Kind of like drought. The day's coming.
The fine critter bouncing on the hill
Aint the same when she's laid low.
Skinned she's awful.
Like the insides of a calving cow.

And you cant blow the spots off a leopard anyhow.

Doll on the Mantelpiece

Here on the mantel where a Dresden doll
Looks into a frozen german hill
All is still, chill, white,
Except the red stain on her lips,
The blood of colour there.

She is poised for a dance above the fire,
A hand out for a partner neither here
Nor anywhere. The fire breathes below
A savage noise of wood and she looks out
Over the white hill, still as a doll,
Chill in her world of ivory.

Why do I think of clowns, of emperors,
Of Nietzsche in his tower and all Berlin
Falling in flames while this silly doll
Stands on a fire, calm beside a frozen hill?

Epilogue

When our mayor was put out to eat grass
And on the street manholes opened like eyes,
Everyone said it had come from below
Because the street was nervous, empty,
And the sewers rumbled for days, the wires
Sang in the high wind and cracks appeared
In the gray cement like folds in an elephant's hide.

Everyone said it had come from below
Because the banks toppled over like great gods
And fire flamed out of the mouth of the stock exchange,
And our bird-like mayor, like a hoofed thing,
Galloped away to the green fields in the country.

from *Black and Secret Man*

Charles Isaac Mandel

Those uplands of the suburban mind,
sunlit, where dwell the lithe ironists,
athletic as greeks, boy-lovers,
mathematical in love as in science.
Formalists. What have I to do with them?
I gather the few relics of my father:
his soiled Tallis, his Tefillin,
the strict black leather of his dark faith.

Day of Atonement: Standing

My Lord, how stands it with me now
who, standing here before you
(who, fierce as you are, are also just),
cannot bow down. You order this.
Why, therefore, I must break
if bend I will not, yet bend I must.

But I address myself to you thus,
covered and alert, and will not bare
my self. Then I must bear you,
heavy as you are.
                        This is the time
the bare tree bends in the fierce wind
and stripped, my God, springs to the sky.

Secret Flower

Sometimes you are a house
sometimes you unfold
ages and ages old
    you are sometimes
    a house with four rooms
    and four kings
    and four queens
secret flower
of my own design.

Deeper and more secret
darker and older
you unfold.

I have watched lovers
drop from your petals
into the room of kings
before the table of judges.

How can this be? It is Sunday.
My children are making paper men
no one has been poisoned
no one has been hung
there is even laughter in the room.

Darker and still more secret
older and unfolded
beyond my designing heart
beyond even my crying out
through your four rooms
past the hanging tree
beyond the swaying lovers
beyond the judges

who is that lying on the green carpet?
who is being carried on the stone tablet?
why do these gesture and posture before me?

I kneel before the four-armed god
gather up the shredded paper heads
and turn toward the suddenly open door.

There Is No One Here Except Us Comedians

1

In what we call dreams I see
a fairground of wheels inside wheels
where I am turned into nobody
nobody's son nobody's daughter

and orphanages
where children
drag toward iron gates yellow dolls
and huge rolling balls
made in the shape of towering fathers

2

I pray nightly for release
I ask of a door shaped like a bat
to fly away with me
I want to be in a wheatfield
stupid as grain yellowing in the sun
I want to be something like a bird,
part reptile, able to stare blankly
for minutes
     at the jade trees
     at the jewelled grass
     the crystal city

whispering blasphemy
I want to walk over the doors of the city
my bird feet tinkling at keyholes

I want you to know I am innocent
I want you to open the last door
into the field of orphan wheat
the orient grain the green golden corn

David

all day the gopher-killing boys
   their sling-shot arms
     their gopher-cries

the king insisting
   my poetry must stop

I have written nothing since May

instead
      walk among the boys
gopher-blood on their stretched
hands
      murder will end murder
the saying goes, someone must
do something about the rodents
and poems do not:
             even the doctors
admit that it's plague
ask me about my arms
        look
at my shadow hanging
   like a slingshot

the world turns like a murderous stone
   my forehead aching with stars

Hebraism

The law is the law and is
terribly Hebrew which is as you
know mostly poems about cooking
and meat to be cured in water and
salt and children to be counted
for pages of generation amid clean
   and also unclean women

A Cage of Oats

To James Reaney and Jay Macpherson

How many prisons do I count?
Here is the wall I first ran from
and here there is a second wall,
the wall I ran against to flee
the first, and here there is a cage.

Inside the cage there is a second cage.
Inside the second cage there is a third.

Inside the third
there is a bird.

A Quaker holds a box of oats
on which a Quaker holds a box.
A mirror mirrors oats
for oats are mirrors of their crops
which farmer-quaker-man will thresh
and eat to put the seeds inside
the Quaker man who holds a box.

There may be stars inside of stones
(or other stones): inside of stars
there may be burning seeds.

What boxed bird so great
it can eat
stone, man, star and seed?

Departure

There was merely a brief note:
"Have seen Edmonton
am leaving at once."
                    I think:
it must have been the buildings
or perhaps the art gallery
or even the university.

But his friends tell me
he had no ambition
his children were slovenly
recently he recovered from a strange disease
he no longer knows what numbers are
nor understands the language spoken here.

Cassandra

This has nothing to do with brothels.

Sometimes it seems my daughter or my wife
or my neighbour's wife, bright-eyed,
imitates an image out of sleep. They walk
as if I had dwindled, looking past me
toward unreasonable parliaments
crouching beside senatorial hills.

I have been practising this poetry in secret.
Also I have made advances toward pregnant women.
But there have been no unusual shadows,
all the swimming pools remain clear of blood,
and by the gates the watcher has not raised his arms.

Rapunzel

Girl in a Tower

Another one of those puzzles
    there's not a farmer
    skinny as a gold seed
    tough as a nutcracker
    can plough or crack.

How do towers grow like that?
    Overnight: the garden
    a green sky, its moon
    like beet, its sun
    a turnip underground?

Many girls lock themselves up,
    become pantries, closets.
    Some, like trees, grow bark,
    and others, like rivers,
    burble into dimpled pools.

But they are not these crooked
    wicked towers, not rooms
    inside of rooms, not brooms
    to thrash out of a seedy man
    his golden crop and garden.

    I lean on a ladder of hair,
    remember the right rhymes,
    look up at the green head,
climb toward the turnip-colour sun.

To My Children

A rose grew in my head
My father lay dead
My mother fell among stones
Two flowers grew in my loins

I sing to my blossoming wife
My father is dead
My mother abandoned her life
Why should I lay down my head

Stony and brittle my days
My children sing psalms
The rabbis are ancient and wise
Blessed by my flowering names

from *An Idiot Joy*

The Meaning of the I CHING

i

unopened
        book of old men
        orange-blossom book
                before me
you were
        how could you contain me?

do you not see I am the mouths
of telegraphs and cemeteries?
my mother groaned like the whole
of Western Union to deliver
my message
        and yelling birthdays
that unrolled from my lungs
like ticker-tape for presidents
about to be murdered
        I sped
on a line that flew
to the vanishing point of the west

before I was
        you were
unopened book
        do not craze me
with the odour of orange-blossom

do not sit there
like smiling old men

        how could you contain me?

ii

under my fingers words form themselves
it's crazy to talk of temples in this day
but light brightens on my page
today moving against the wooden house
all shapes change yet stay
as if they were marble in autumn
as if in the marbled yellow autumn
each western house becomes a shrine
stiff against the age of days
under my fingers stiffly formed

one cannot be another, I cry,

I will walk in streets that vanish
noting peculiar elms like old women
who will crash under the storm of sun
that breaks elm, woman, man
into a crumble of stump and bark
until the air is once more clear
in the sane emptiness of fall

iii

my body speaks to me
as my arms say: two are one
as my feet say: earth upon earth
as my knees say: bow down, unhinge yourself
as my cells say: we repeat the unrepeatable

the book speaks: arrange yourself in the form
that will arrange you

before I was: colours that hurt me
arranged themselves in me

before I was: horizons that blind me
arranged themselves in me

before I was: the dead who speak to me
arranged themselves in me

iv

I am the mouths
of smiling old men

there rises from me
the scent of orange-blossoms

I speak in the words
of the ancient dead

arranged
in the raging sun
in the stiffening age of days

and in the temple of my house

one becomes another

The Milk of Paradise

1

Marvel upon marvel the berries of the sun
inflame the tumbling waters of my limbs
I am given to such visions: wide-eyed
luminous men walk through a hairy land
toward a milky glade where goats bleat

2

I put away this last unfinished poem
to think with trouble of a friend
who wrote me and whose words I scorned

Streetlights

they're not sunflowers
yet they burn on their stems
like the golden eyes of those other plants

and they bend
in such an iron complaint
toward the street's inverted sky

I'd like to think
they know as much of final things
as any living creature who endures the dark.

The Trance of Poetry

My children frightened, I quarrel with my wife,
And all that passes through my raging mind,
This poem I must write
                         lovers, entranced,
Will whisper mouth to mouth my lines

I put the difficulty down to god
Who failed to be unambiguous in such matters

In the Fifty-seventh Century of Our Lord

semitic and secret I plan new evasions,
survival, the tribal rite
                     to be
horribly chummy with god
as if he cared
                  in particular
about my politics
my plans for adultery
my marvellous scheme to blame it
on my neighbour's blameless wife

Girl on a High Wire

Do you think I'd sit here staring
if I knew how to invent chair-lifts
or lacked this odd taste for vertigo?

What if I dare you to jump, saying, ah
my hurt bird, I will catch you—
and if I weren't there (someone calling,
my son pointing at camels or wanting
to pee) when your eyes became horizons?
Or if you fell
into the well of bankers, mid-wives,
my brother-in-law, the Prudential Life
Insurance Company?
                    I see them,
heroine, hefting you, their applause
ringing your head with the clatter of zircons,
mouths blowing little balloons of praise.

The great globe circles.
Soldiers fall into muddy rivers.
Boys walk the tightrope of their prison yard.

I can no longer look at telephone wires,
the vanishing point of your unfinished portrait.

I shall devote myself to entomology,
practise weight-lifting with dinky toys,
but who will keep me from my crooked prayers,
those mad doves that fling haloes around you?

Houdini

I suspect he knew that trunks are metaphors,
could distinguish between the finest rhythms
unrolled on rope or singing in a chain
and knew the metrics of the deepest pools

I think of him listening to the words
spoken by manacles, cells, handcuffs,
chests, hampers, roll-top desks, vaults,
especially the deep words spoken by coffins

escape, escape: quaint Harry in his suit
his chains, his desk, attached to all attachments
how he'd sweat in that precise struggle
with those binding words, wrapped around him
like that mannered style, his formal suit

and spoken when? by whom? What thing first said
"there's no way out?"; so that he'd free himself,
leap, squirm, no matter how, to chain himself again,
once more jump out of the deep alive
with all his chains singing around his feet
like the bound crowds who sigh, who sigh.

The Silences

1

like a blank page
            unused
I could write anything:
everything
           you've no
way of knowing what
I might say
         think
what whispers
before any word spoken

think
     all is possible
do you dare
think of the possible silences?

2

the marvellous gods are silent
their wide eyes baffle us

we cannot read their eyes
their impractical calm gestures

in the remote hills
they walk
         noiseless
their footsteps

3

before the possibility
it was impossible

syllables
       I think of your mouth

4

throttles splendid utterance
the unspoken

gathers in harvests

5

when he put out his eyes
he said: I have said everything

you will not hear my voice again

6

what I said became

7

a letter: don't read this
so that what I've said
might not become
                    anyhow
let us perplex our hearts
with uselessness

8

think only of the unwritten
all
   a shrine
          of possible

          silences

Manner of Suicide

Man, says Menninger, against himself:

"hanging themselves
taking poison in the top of high trees
throwing themselves on swiftly revolving circular saws
exploding dynamite in their mouths
thrusting red hot pokers down their throats
hugging red hot stoves
freezing to death on piles of ice
in refrigerator cars
lacerating their throats on barbed wire fences
drowning themselves head downwards in barrels
suffocating themselves head downwards in chimneys
diving into white-hot coke ovens
throwing themselves into craters of volcanoes
shooting themselves with ingenious combinations
of a rifle and a sewing machine
strangling themselves with their hair
swallowing poisonous spiders
piercing their hearts with corkscrews and
darning needles
cutting their throats with handsaws and sheepshears
hanging themselves with grape vines
swallowing strips of underclothing and buckles
of suspenders
forcing teams of horses to tear their heads off
drowning themselves in vats of soft soap
plunging into retorts of molten glass
jumping into slaughter-house tanks of blood
decapitation with homemade guillotines
self-crucifixion"
"the archaic symbolism of the psychotic"
"The Cremation of Sam McGee"
"the undisturbed bliss of inter-uterine
  existence illustrated by fantasies in
  the Bible, poetry, casual conversation
  of the man on the street, the church hymnal,
  newspapers, patients, the writings of Shelley
  and Freud"

EVENING SERVICE FOR THE SABBATH: THANKSGIVING FOR GOD'S
UNFAILING MERCIES:
> We will give thanks unto Thee and declare
> Thy praise for our lives which are committed
> unto Thy hand, and for our souls which are in
> Thy charge, and for Thy miracles which are
> daily with us, and for Thy wonders and Thy
> benefits, which are wrought at all times,
> evening, morn, and noon.

Woodbine

When a crooked man meets beauty
You think there'd be shouting in the streets

I wish there were no allegories
I wish the doctors could do something about my forked tongue

Believe me, I have gone about with pails on my head
so that my friends would recognize me.

Lord, Lord, pollution everywhere
But I breathe still
         and breathless, sweet
woodbine, colour of honey, touches my skin
as if my unbelieving eyes made no difference at all

House of Candy

Larches charred still leaning in the swamp,
I stumble here. What do I know of muskeg?
Woodsmen I have met in stories saved young girls.
It was the smoking hearts of casual rodents
They threw before the queen, her clouded eyes.

If I go forward to the blackened tower,
What must I learn about this offering?
How in my bloodless hands will I take blood
Or how appease the queen, her unencumbered arms?

Hunters darkened stare through sullen smoke
As if to see my shape where larches stand
Or find me in the smouldering stump of pine
Or like some candied house, a crystal rock,
Or marvellous and abstract in a cave,
All bearded whisper and prophetic eye.

They do not know how at the story's end,
Duller than prose, I turned toward the south,
Sought out the urgent maiden, warned her of the queen,
Then drove my knife into her heart to save a passing rat.

The Speaking Earth

grandfathers fall into it
their mighty beards muffled in grass

and admirals, the sea-sounding men

lovers fall into the earth
like rain on wet dark bodies

listen, our lady earth flowers
into the sea-green language
of grass and drowned admirals

listen: in bearded branches
clasped like broken hands
admiring birds
lovers singing of their kiss
before and after all the words

From the North Saskatchewan

when on the high bluff discovering
the river cuts below
                 send messages
we have spoken to those on the boats

I am obsessed by the berries they eat
all night odour of Saskatoon
and an unidentifiable odour
something baking
                the sun
never reaches the lower bank

I cannot read the tree markings
today the sky is torn by wind:
a field after a long battle
strewn with corpses of cloud

give blessings to my children
speak for us to those who sent us here
say we did all that could be done
we have not learned
what lies north of the river
or past those hills that look like beasts

The Moon in All Her Phases

I'd say, in the old manner:
she imagines our existence,
its changes, illusions

well, luminous times are gone
most of my friends quarrel
drink
        are not, though satyrs,
lordly
        recently one in rage
told me he loved the first war
because they sang such songs

we grope toward each other
hands fumble among clothes

I cant remember:
                did your eyes
your body glow?
                I cant remember
the difficult lovely words.

Listen, the Sea

yes what is
I'm learning

by your leave
leaving
            rising
to leave
            return
and turn
            we
deliberate
by the waves
rhythm casual
move
        tidal
as
        traffic
as
    the sea-women

neither are they
certain uncertain
but with us
            withal
within
        their song
here
    oh hear
it is

Marina

Because she spoke often of the sea we thought she had
   known another country, her people distant, not
   forgotten

We did not know then who was calling her or what songs
   she listened to or why the sea-birds came to rest
   upon her long fingers

Or why she would shudder like a sea-bird about to take
   flight, her eyes changing with the changing light

As the sea-changing opal changes, as a shell takes its
   colours from the sea as if it were the sea

As if the great sea itself were held in the palm of your hand

They say the daughters of the sea know the language of birds,
   that in their restless eyes the most fortunate learn
   how the moon rises and sets

We do not know who is calling her or why her eyes change
   or what shore she will set her foot upon

from *Stony Plain*

Wabamun

1

lake
   holds
         sun moon stars

       trees
          hold

stars moon sun

2

thunder
     and sky
towel
     wet sand
in yellow light

     yesterday

3

on water
many suns
      here there
fires then
silent comedians
gulls
perch jumping

4

only
   waves   motion
   sun   dancing

no   sun

only
   light
hurting
in its
    endless
dance

5

each day I
step
   farther
into dark water

once I will
know
   no longer

whether
     that one
floating
    is myself
or the light
      one
standing
     on the red
pier

6

moon train on causeway

coal cars

    a white moon

7

to have come to this
simplicity
        to know
only
   the absolute
calm
     lake

    before

    night

8

clover   smell
sweet stars in a green sky

white sweet stars
blossom in a green sky

clover   stars
in a white sky

white
     stars

At Wabamun the Calgary Power Station

leans white in the moon
light puts white slabs up
light shanty whiteness leans

as if it owned the land

daytime horses crop grass
unknowing transformers hum

transformers at the word
it takes on fiery hair
blazing it transmits
messages furious and hairy
it sends and receives from stars
ancient planets   people
who speak like horses new words

then sparks perform dead
parabolas and loops die
fireplace quietens it is
morning it is light only
the power the power hums

and the lake grows green
again in sunlight

                    it is
morning algae and weeds
thicken
          the green lake
wobbles
            we look at
each other   alien forms

Edmonton, 1967

as if by Colville
I mean "hard edge"
stucco   white wall
gravel &
         legs
in one direction shadows
leaning midget
above the pavement narrows
rapid as the river
               everything
disappears
        neatness: axiomatic
        houses   here
now gone
        "You are impatient
with poetry" my friend writes
from Iceland

Two Dream Songs for John Berryman

1

Henry, it says to me here
you took yourself to a bridge.
And you, weary and wavery,
walked, bone and brain, all
to the rail
        there perched
waved farewell from rail

Is that how it was done?

Is it only possible to live
how we have done backwards
dreaming our way from death to
bony life?
        Well, it was gaily
done
    but, here on the coast of Spain,
heartsick   like   you
                and hurt too
by burning poems that will not write
themselves I
        say
now fare-you-well
with Sylvia, Ted, Randall,
and all your hurt friends,

God notwithstanding

2

It is done but not done well
Henry to betake yourself to ice
and death in a Minnesota morning

or a bruise
throwing yourself from bridge
to ice
        why would you want so
to say to me or to God once more
that nothing is fair
among fair women and hardy men

to God
        who never once cared
now name him as you will

it's both night and day
not done well to you or anyone
less or better
                not well

Rembrandt

blunt
    he knew
solidities
       darkness
light
    all those men
    in "The Night Watch"

what they saw
in the nooks of their view

but why then
the apostle's style

and why
     the Jewish bride
untouched
      her groom
handling her breast

her lower gown

redder than the darkest ruby?

Autobiography

every night I dream I have
wakened to find someone else
has written and published
my autobiography
made of tapes of my own voice
in words I have never spoken

Don Quixote Writes to His Priest

neither their books nor magicians
offer harm to our person or travellers

once a skinned rabbit alarmed us
as did a lamb's head chucked on the road
all its flesh wounded and
but one eye remarking sadly
the quick feet of passing men

they flavour their tea with shiba
mint leaves, rough sugar in lumps,
take it with almond cakes

nothing in their medinas offends

yet each night someone pours smoking
dreams into my ears and nostrils

when my mouth opens
only arabic scribbles emerge

who turns my folded thoughts
back and forth
the pages of an unreliable book?

Oscar Wilde

my warden stares counting again
clenched anxieties
                         worn
arguments crumbling reassurances
I've stolen from my day's ration

he looks oddly at the rose-red city
ruined inside my head
                         he measures
gaps opened by earthquakes in my skull

later he will prod at pigs
turn over one by one dazed hungers
squirming desires

would you now say to my people
the poems were worth it?

take these coins for my children
say after
            it was art I cared for
despised life

Saskatchewan Surveyor

at a correction line
he reads the wind's grammar

rhetoric falls from trees

in a simple sentence of land
a disappointed syntax

For Ann: On the Question of Franco's Successor

above me three ochre terraces
olive trees design another cliff
amid concrete, wood, new apartments
workmen sing flamenco   casual
passionate
         ochre land
              red
land   slate mountains
yellow birds   day
sky   yellow as a finch
moon   look
a whitewashed house on a hill

is a great leap forward necessary
are fortunes to be made at a red bridge

we have felt our own colour, skin
in sun morning and moon night and

satisfied (we say) we see
land   sea

knowledge no longer a burden

we know freedom
         songs

Earthworms Eat Earthworms and Learn

as with Aunt Adeline
the one with the large bosom
one of the complicated cousins
who on a hot Regina afternoon
wept at a hurt finger
and thrust into her vagina
other fingers

so eating one another worm
knows inside another worm
the square root Adeline knew
and cousins knowing cousins
uncles uncles
aunts aunts

it goes on
wisdom of cells

this rod dividing into that
rod into that code that code

so it was with Aunt Eda
who coded Uncle Lou
who had himself been coded

into

and father knew father
mothering the last of the jews
who on the Hirsch land
put in new seeds
and new codes
and new aunts

so we survived
but had become
being as
we were

solutions

the seed

the new seed

final solution

remember forever the neon
Orpheum (?) Winnipeg 1935
lights exploding liquid
oh the elegant lobby
uncles and lights lights lights
then
      film

Locality

new year's eve my friend from Utah
remarks a cubist view of our village
from his apartment
                      church
pine tree
        white tilted homes

"our village" I said

it was the need for art
made me greedy about lives
knowing nothing of their homes
or for that matter
              our own

but it was cold
our children made loud noise
driving out even these desperate spirits

late   alone   I remembered
it was not Spain but Estevan,
that home, I meant

Agatha Christie

being civil she saw poison
as a flaw in character
the use of a knife
a case history in Freud

difficult to explain
her dislike of jews

or why night upon night
she plotted solutions
to deaths she must have dreamed

her 200,000,000 readers
how much longing for murder
the neatness of England
is and still remains

though in Belfast, say,
bombs have other reasons
and no one explains

Message from Saturn

I have not forgotten
their camps   ovens
electronic dentists curators
surgeons newspapers genital
prongs their devices

now the unmemory
the forgetting

knowing this witness
no other testimony

see they approach
children not knowing

how the planet burned
from what star strangers came
their eyes their helmets
mask of turtle

children my children
welcome them
sing war songs old songs

Chief Dan Kennedy

when he was eighty
anthropology
impressed him
also memory

now at one hundred
he remembers
his dark wife
her silence

night night
what reason
what delight
either bed
or waking
could excuse

and down there
yes there the same
village whores
his people ours

he showed me
past
    English journals
with maps
pictures of Indians

On the Death of Ho Chi Minh

toward the end
he became frail as rice paper
his beard whispering thin ideograms

how unlike the great carved storm
that was Marx's face
                           how unlike
the darkness and fury
in Beethoven's head
                           scarcely
anything to be consumed

bombs destroy   destroy
you cannot touch his body now
or burn his poems

First Political Speech

first, in the first place, to begin with, secondly,
in the second place, lastly

again, also, in the next place, once more, moreover,
furthermore, likewise, besides, similarly, for example,
for instance, another

then, nevertheless, still, however, at the same time,
yet, in spite of that, on the other hand, on the contrary

certainly, surely, doubtless, indeed, perhaps, possibly,
probably, anyway, in all probability, in all likelihood,
at all events, in any case

therefore, consequently, accordingly, thus, as a result,
in consequence of this, as might be expected

the foregoing, the preceding, as previously mentioned

as already stated

> Transition Table
> from *Learning to Write* by Ernest H. Winter (Second
> Revised Edition) Macmillan (Toronto, 1961), p.156

On the 25th Anniversary of the Liberation of Auschwitz: Memorial Services, Toronto, January 25, 1970 YMHA Bloor & Spadina

the name is hard
a German sound made out of
the gut guttural throat
y scream yell ing open
voice mouth growl
                 and sweat
"the only way out of Auschwitz
is through the chimneys"
                     of course
that's second hand   that's told
again   Sigmund Sherwood (Sobolewski)
twisting himself into that sentence
before us on the platform
                    the poem
shaping itself late in the after
noon later than it would be:

Pendericki's "Wrath of God"
moaning electronic Polish theatric
the screen silent
               framed by the name
looking away from/pretending not there
no   name   no   not   name no

      Auschwitz
     in GOTHIC lettering
             the hall
a parody a reminiscence a nasty memory
the Orpheum in Estevan before Buck Jones
the Capitol in Regina before Tom Mix
waiting for the guns
waiting for the cowboy killers
one two three
         Legionnaires
Polish ex-prisoners Association
Legions
     their medals their flags

so the procession, the poem gradual
ly insistent beginning to shape itself
with the others
                    walked with them
into the YMHA Bloor & Spadina
thinking apocalypse shame degradation
thinking bones and bodies melting
thickening thinning melting bones and bodies
thinking not mine / must speak clearly
the poet's words / Yevtyshenko at Baba-Yar

there this January snow
heavy wet the wind heavy wet
the street grey white slush melted concrete
bones and bodies melting slush
                                        saw
with the others
                    the prisoner
in the YMHA hall Bloor & Spadina
arms wax stiff body stiff unnatural
coloured face blank eyes
                                walked
with the others toward the screen
toward the picture
                    SLIDES
            this is mother
            this is father
            this is
                    the one who is
waving her arms like that
is the one who
                    like
I mean running with her breasts bound
ing
      running
                    with her hand here and there
with her here and
                        there
hands
      that   that is
the poem becoming the body
becoming the faint hunger

ing body
          prowling
                    through
words the words words the words
opening   mouths ovens
the generals smiling saluting
in their mythic uniforms god-like
generals uniforms with the black leather
with the straps and the intricate leather
the phylacteries and the prayer shawl
corsets and the boots and the leather straps

and the shining faces of the generals in their boots
and their stiff wax bodies their unnatural faces
and their blank eyes and their hands their stiff hands
and the generals in their straps and wax and stiff
staying standing
                    melting bodies and thickening
                    quick flesh on flesh handling
                    hands
     the poem flickers, fades
the four Yarzeit candles guttering one
     each four million lights dim
my words drift
               smoke from chimneys and ovens
     a bad picture, the power failing
   pianist clattering on and over and through
the long Saturday afternoon in the Orpheum
     while the whitehatted star spangled cowboys
        shot the dark men and shot the dark men
        and we threw popcorn balls and grabbed
        each other and cheered:
                              me jewboy yelling
for the shot town and the falling men
     and the lights come on
                         and
     with the others
standing in silence

the gothic word hangs
over us on a shroud-white screen

and we drift away
to ourselves
to the late Sunday Times
the wet snow
the city

a body melting

The President and the Chairman Meet

1

when great men greet each other
with tea and wine and ceremony
small ones draw close
to guard themselves

2

there will be storms
as ever nightfall only
much later moon rising

3

drunkenness, prison, disgrace
a bad book of poems
who distinguishes?

two hundred years old the olive trees
twist under time no worse than ours

4

so many deeds cry out to be done
only the hour waits
the chairman
and the congress senators
before our great leap forward
before we find again the same
almond trees   the same moon

Political Speech

(for PET)

think: planets turn
            moons come into phase and out again
            tiny spanish birds rise to their own songs
            night comes and goes
            in the heavens constellations wheel
            and this man speaks

                    (beyond form
                        words like gyres
                        like Kubrick's great
                            globe
                  its weltschmerz

                  voices   voices

                  at night they come to me
                  disguised as clowns
                  or in their sinister form
                  as policemen, sisters
                  asking me again
                  to plunge down
                  a great elevator
                  to take a merry-go-round
                  whose legs are silk pants

                        a sewer in my throat

but there are no voices
inside or outside this poem
neither a poem nor an opera
you said
        we're losing this now
it no longer makes sense
it isn't going to work

thesis: freedom
antithesis: necessity

if the revolution was about to occur
would the people of quebec rise up

the people of quebec would rise up

therefore the revolution was about to occur

wrong again
it goes another way:
                            since
you always did as I said
                            washed
your speeches wiped your rhetoric
clean as the parsing in your prose
looked after the creases in your biology
and the intertrigo in your quadrivium
you drew the following circles in the air:

                    the nation is rational

                                        (wrong)

                    america is either good or bad

                                        (equally wrong)

                    canada is either possible or not

                                        (still wrong)

and the possibility?

                    only that we are older
                    and awake
                                or not

Political Science

(after Brecht and Trudeau)

in the cartoon by Groz
lechery   greed
                    those
outlines: spiritual beings

and here   the same vomit
chips lager iconic tits

there's your new nation
one juridical
                    and free

Cabinet Secrets

1

privy to secrets I'm giving this one
away free: Canadian Daniel Ellsberg
with 47 volumes of our own genuine Pentagon Papers
(secretly I've yearned to be an anarchist
enemy of the state, traitor, political prisoner
Clifford Irving
                    at night I dream of
half-naked girls running through streets,
Stratford, Estevan, Yellow Grass, Corrinne)

I know the senior civil servant
who at 4:00 am in cold October
carried to the Governor General who
I think had not yet run his usual three
miles before breakfast the war measures
act to be signed
                    once he showed me
the cabinet room the table where

ministers sit where the prime minister
sits where the civil servant sits at
a secretary's table of eighteenth-century
but it is especially maple or walnut or
curved and I know where he must have written
war measures

2

so it has been always
archangels with great golden eyes
you cannot look at   those aloof hands
those golden tables
                    listen: I have heard
they do secret studies they have profiles
so finally I think angels come to a hole
in the ground inside a house inside a farm

with aloof hands
they make coffins
photographs

they take the guns of revelation

terror dug out of the ground
like wet mice
                    disappears
in the eternal silence

the cabinet

From "The Pentagon Papers"

Glossary:

			EPTEL	
AA	CAT	DIA	(Deptel/Septel?)	
AAA	CHICOM	DOD		
AID	CHINAT			FAL
ASA	CHMAAG			FAR
ABM	CIAP			FEC
AMB	CINCPAC			FMWA
ASAP	COMUSMACV			FY
				FYI
		LOC	MAAG	PACON
ICA			MAC	POLAD
ICC	KIA		MAP	
I			MDAP	QTE
IDA				
ISA				

ROK RSM RSSZ RTA RVNAF RVNA   SACSAMSAR
SMMSNIESTCSVNTAORTERMTETTFTO&ETRIMUNO
USAFUSGUSIAUSIBUSISUSOMUWVCVMVNVNAFVOA
WTYT
     UNQTE
        ROLLING THUNDER

        BARREL ROLL

BLUE SPRINGS FARMGATE FLAMING DART LEAPING LENA

The Trilemma:
    a. Will-breaking strikes on the North (para 7) are
balked by (1) flash-point limits, (2) by doubts
that DRV will cave and (3) by doubts that VC will
obey caving DRV
    b. Large U.S. troop deployments. (para 9) are blocked
by "French-defeat" and "Korea" syndromes, and Quat is
queasy. (Troops could be net negatives, and be beseiged).
    c. Exit by negotiations (para 9) is tainted by the
humiliation likely to follow.

insurrection defection dissension impotence defeat-
ism concession accommodation

    deployment of Frogs and Sams in North Vietnam
    hot pursuit flak suppression strike strikes strikes
risks:
    losses panic revulsion sympathetic fires over
    Berlin, Cyprus, Kashmir, Jordan waters

      stretch-out retard the program
      circuit breaker

           shunt

Sea Things: Nerja

this poem is built to
see through

        see through

this poem

      see

through

      it

is

   nothing

      nothing

is this poem see

through

     over and
over   I said
nothing
    no one
believed
    me

or the poem
       not

there

   see

The Garden of Delights

and so we went down to the river
to the corpses there but on our way
beside a willow copse we heard ring-
ing sounds as if a tree were hung
with bells and looked to see the willow
blossom into crystal as if its leaves
were birds
        so from the branches hung
lovers copulate their loves dropping
into a giant pool where storks and emus
swam with copulating lovers in their wings
while from their eggs emerged the limbs
of love and lovers clasping legs about
crystal goblets, bells and some stroked
flutes that blew sweet music from their
assholes while others sucked the tongues
of birds being fucked by mice or toads
or long-eared sages whose bald heads
served service to young balding girls
their legs entwined about the sage's eyes
and all went circling round the pool
of love
     now
       two such bodies will
not be seen again
        love dear
in them life dear in them

so I looked at corpses, noticing
three female death still coy in them
and thought the whole world is a coffin
and a bed
      and watched the river wash
blood over a dark city near the top
(or bottom) left of Bosch's tryptich

Velasquez: Las Meninas

1

change the lines about
stone man and stone moon
to read   reflect on images

(fish locked in ice
a memory of summer)

since form longs to be free
and not to know its name

just so
        Velasquez put him-
self into Las Meninas creat-
ing not only "a theology
of painting"
                but self:

(if he is
        there who
painted the picture?

Gautier: "but where is the
picture?")
                neither anecdot-
al nor deceitful
                measured

as if in that court your
life "saved" depended on

style: looking "as if"

so that Dona Margarita looks
out as deformed Maria Barbola
looks out
        at (being looked at
by The Maids in Waiting) Felipe?

Mariana? who look into a mirror
looking out at you looking at
them
     as if
       I hadn't saved the
poem from the moon stone

and the stone man

         2

if he is looking at the
picture he could not have
painted it
     if he isn't
how could he have painted
it
  if he painted it
where was he
        if he is
in it

         3

"We observe the artist is
not painting on the canvas
which we as spectators are
viewing"
      Complete Guide
      to the Prado etc.

         4

reflect: if he is
not painting that
painting

         5

"calculating the real
existence of atmosphere"

Envoi

my country is not a country
                                but winter
rivers of ice
from St. Hubert terrible knives
run through the whiteness of my veins

politics pierce my heart
on a floor littered with history
I shiver while wardens shovel in
lunatic sentences, rag upon rag

it must be cold in prison, in québec

and your heart hurt singer
what do you see through its pane

icy slaves circle the river
montréal tense against the steel of its manacles
your words drifting   frozen wounds
                                          blessing
a sick bride
a murderous bridegroom
                          that wedding
whose children will be colder killers
than the words of this or any other song

from *Out of Place*

I

The Return

the return:

in the estevan poem, for example,
how every one can be seen eating
or is it reading
                but not everyone
there is myself in the souris valley
forty years later
                    Ann
looking at wild flowers
cactus   their thick colours

I remember how I dreamt
her
        pale as a flower
        in the white sun
and in the dream
she is taking pictures

she photographs me
walking away
along a curving path
the flowers coloured
                and
my father appears
my mother appears
saying no words
troubled
                and all
the ghostly jews
of estevan
                    praying

in the synagogue
    of the valley
in the covenant
    of coal mines
in these pictures
    of estevan

signs:

and omens   windows
facing inward
         "an ideal
inserted into the plane
we call reality"   words
warning this is the place
you reach
     to name
remember and recite

whatever has been hidden here
remains of speech
        the town lives
in its syntax we are ghosts

look   on the road beyond
mesas and moonscape
hoodoos   signs cut in rock
graffiti   gods
an indescribable border

doors of perception:

    roads lead here   there
on the prairie Ann holds the Pinto
along great swoops of highway down
from Lloydminster past Batoche
rebellion Rudy's book researched
prophetic voices as a guide

in Huxley's version time curves
upon itself
             cities of the mescal dream
turned biblical   jeweled places
palaces of John in Revelation
Blake's engraving the drunkenness
of Smart's madness   prophecy

our history is in motion   curved
like straight correction lines
earth-measured on a western grid
place known through time   time
measuring place
             Thompson walked
through unafraid for knowing
measurement and lore
                ignorant
of clocks and vision we accelerate
a sweep through dying towns and farms

now is the badlands   measure
our choices random we believe
whatever we can find or where the map
of our own voices leads us listening to

the road to the cancer clinic
past the sundial's didacticism
toward the language of shadows
bedlam the alcoholic's nightmare
uses of wheat and rye and mould

strict farms die
beside the rails the roads

the sons construct
the rules of mind

the jewish exodus from shtetl to the plains
leads to this eygpt abraham learned
dream-sickness and the way to heal
a place of bread and chemistry

madness is neither east nor north
Riel was hung in streets
I walked on every day to school

birthmark:

seeing a mouse
my mother struck her temple

he'll be marked at birth
she said
       the women cried

I carry the souris
on my brow
       the river
in my head
       the valley
of my dreams
still echoes
with her cry

badlands:

1

black against sky
four horses   simple
particulars   amid
the endless treachery
that is remembering

there are no definitions

2

neither difficult nor easy
crossings
        happen
it appears

3

understand this
simplicity
this land is
treacherous

between Hirsch and
Hoffer
        it is
plain

4

neither difficult nor easy
crossings
        appear
it happens

5

four horses   amid
the endless treachery
that is remembering

desire

near hirsch a jewish cemetery:

ann is taking pictures again
while I stand in the uncut grass
counting the graves: there are forty
I think
        the Hebrew puzzles me
the wind moving the grass
over the still houses of the dead

from the road a muffled occasional
roar   cars passing   no one there
casts a glance at the stone trees
the unliving forest of Hebrew graves

in the picture I stand arms outstretched
as if waiting for someone
                        I am
in front of the gates you can see
the wind here   the grass
always bending the stone unmoved

slaughterhouse:

> after the morning in the slaughterhouse
> grandfather leading me back to the kitchen
> the farm unpainted weathered grandmother
> milking guts of shit for skins and kishke
> it's not a place for boys she says
> her face redder than strawberries
> her hands like cream

lost place:

> in the book of years
> berner told me could be found
> your own name exactly spelled
> his own his sons the russian
> names of villages and jews
>
> twelve strangled ducklings
>
> you were written
>
> I read the land for records now
>
> wild strawberries   cocoa-butter
> taste of Hirsch
>   bags of curdling
> warm spent streams
>
> tested on a hair of berner's beard
> the ritual slaughter knife
>
> even the blood has disappeared

estevan, 1934:

remembering the family we
called breeds   the Roques
their house smelling of urine
my mother's prayers before
the dried fish she cursed
them for their dirtiness their
women I remember too
                                    how
seldom they spoke and
they touched one another

even when the sun killed
cattle and rabbis
                        even
in poisoned slow air
like hunters
                    like lizards
they touched   stone
they touched
                    earth

lines for an imaginary cenotaph:

george hollingdale
bruce carey
george chapman
jacob barney mandel

William Tell Mandel: sd
Capt A.W. (ab) Hardy

Isaac Berner
                    Annie's
son

all the kinds of war
we say our kaddish for

chief Dan Kennedy
singing
beneath the petroglyphs
hoodoos we sd
at Roche Percée

Assiniboine songs

returning from war:
  (for jbm 1918-1944)

        floors gleaming in the white frame house
        yellow as wax the night before he died
        she said her eyes yellow as a hawk's
        she saw him dressed in white   clean
        she said this in the room   the blinds
        drawn   heat leaning on the house
        over the room's dusk the floor's gleam
        white   he was so clean

        in the estevan summer
        hazardous as desert hear
        gopher squeaks momentary hawks
        lean in the pushing and shoving
        wind   the sun breathing
        heat
            and the impossibility of death

petroglyphs at st. victor:

1

watching the sun
watching the sun's wheel
great slow metaphors
wheel toward me out of the sun

they take my eyes from my head
they place my eyes on rocks
they take my crying tongue
they wheel back toward the sun
their black hands carrying my name

now my drawings of god
look no better than my child's
drawing of me
     I remember
the sun his arms flailing
wheat and skin his mouth
warning of hollows and gulleys
one eye grinning news
about crossings
      I try feet now
get the toes wrong
forget the signals once again

whether the snake's head
points inside or outside the sun
for circling the snake ridge
I've always been wrong
about metaphors
about the five figures
of discourse
     the seventy
names of rhetoric and tree
alphabets
    when they gave me
my name I knew the only one
to follow me would mistake

my image/sign
         all the others
praising the gods

2

the crooked gods:

do they mean anything?
I ask Ann
       parkland
rolling below sandstone

silent
     she turns
the camera
       here
there
     I kneel
before the crooked gods

last light wheeling
over the land
their handprints
their great feet
their stone faces
move
     turning
we leave
take with us
photographs
silent
    as
their open mouths

3

Point Alison
where the super-continental stands
our children cry out
barely glimpse redness a form
the end of names and aesthetics

later
amid wreckage of slippers
licorice I remember the cut
god's mouths at Wood Mountain
rhetoric of stone its bluntness

Ann
talking
about children
tomorrow
our return
home
train time

the hoffer colony:

just as in McCourt's *Saskatchewan*
though unlike his prose
clapboard buildings on a ridge
pastel fields tree stumps
an overturned quebec heater
iron bedstead rusting
useless springs
     the clichés
appalling over-written
like a bad travel book

and in a concrete vault its floor
littered with prairie I find
scripture a farmer's exodus Israel
Hoffer's accounting I begin
to feel gloomy about possibilities
in mythology some books of the bible
devote themselves to family lines
some to a census
      there are stories
about passionate heroic tax
collectors others where merchants
ruined by investment sell children

I look uneasily at grain inventories
machinery bills, newspapers
think about my uncle standing
among rocks with Israel
both Jews proud and successful

before we take our easy leave
how should we understand
prophecies and miracles?

II

The Double

the doppelganger:

ways to prevent me:

refusing to be interrupted especially by children
single-mindedness to the point of brutality
in all matters of politics religion metaphysics &
the character and lives of your closest friends
praising the worst lines of your fellow writers
jogging followed by volley ball and cold showers
concentrated masturbation before and after sex
sleeping with a towel knotted in your back
inspired teaching ferocious tactics in rumoli
combinations of alcohol librium and bad novels

seeing I'm here you know all methods fail
you don't even know how long it has been
what I might have said to children or others
now it's forever too late
no one could possibly know
you've been gone for days
when I make love to your wife
she will moan and praise you
asking you never to leave

where shall I say you have gone?

doubles: estevan

the Orpheum shows a desert film
in Ann's picture the Orpheum is pale
against a paler sunlight a washed-out
film: someone who could be me stands
beside a sweet shop that the Mathers ran
for boys whose faces had been ruined

on such illusions we have built our lives
palaces of art where Sara dreams
her precious dream of being
                                            all that
every image makes impossible and true

licorice whips and jawbreakers
that sweetness of the tongue mocks
broken faces of the ones returned
like images of films we fled
the hunchback lobster monster
broken patched
                        I stand
inside the film and stare
at places that I never knew

questions a double asks:

whether anything in your dreams accounts for
   his appearing now
how it is the explanation of acute anxiety does
   not suffice to dispel him
what in your philosophical readings could be
   consistent with the notion of reduplication
whether he is a refutation of clock time and a
   way to justify eternity
why you are afraid of him as shown by your
   blood pressure and pulse

does his appearance improve your sexual
   performance
has the government of Canada Ontario Alberta
   significantly changed because of his presence
what explanations you offer to your father/to
   your department chairman/to the department of revenue
give a detailed account of all sado-masochistic
   fantasies you entertain
refer to each scatalogical childhood incident
   coprophilia necrophilia sodomy

do you know yourself

have you any reason for hope or delight

why do you think I am here

will you change your life

account for the difference between the spider
   and the spider plant

have you considered the fern the coleus the
   philodendron the patience plant the flowers
   the hoya the lilies of the day the ants bees
   sweetness light the sun the moon

why are you writing out these questions

will you do nothing to help me

is poetry all you have to offer

the double world:

it is variously believed that this world is the
double of another, as in Plato, Swedenborg, Malebranche,
some of Immanuel Kant, Arthur C. Clarke, Isaac Asimov,
Stanley Kubrick
                  Two clocks set at the same time in
identical universes should stop at the same time.
This clock is a shadow of that real clock. When I
look at my clock I have no way of knowing whether I am in
the first or second universe. It is spring there too:
and the other Ann has grown an avocado exactly the same
height, greenness, number of leaves as the one Ann grew
here or there. My grandfather Berner weighed the same
in both universes, sang sweet Jewish psalms, ate sour
curds. In the two graveyards Annie Berner is dead.
Nothing on either prairie changes though the winds blow
across immensities your heart would shrivel to imagine
knowing they pass between the worlds and can be heard to do
so on the road to Wood Mountain. That is what was written
in the rocks.

instructions:
(on the nature of doubles and doubling)

    all mirrors should be covered
do not look deeply into a sink of hot water
ditto cold
wear rings on only two fingers
your eyes are doubles doubled
everything divides by two or is uneven
poetry consists in the doubling of words
doubled words are poetic words
this is the true meaning of duplicity
each poem speaks to another poem
the language of poetry is a secret language
these are the true doubles

false doubles are ones and threes
four is a good number

doubled names are: eli   elijah
                            jesse   jesus
                            paul   saul
                            joseph pharoah
                                              etc.

in Hebrew this is common
no one knows the jewish name of god
indian names are secret
poetry is the naming of secret names
among these are:
                god
                spirit
                alphabets

                names in stone
                doubled names
                the psalms
                hoodoos
                animals
                eyes
                jewels

the place of no shadows called badlands
the place of shadows called badlands
you begin to see the difficulties

III

A Suite for Ann

Strange Places

the places that we go are strange
but stranger that we go to place
our strangeness where we neither
know we were nor where but only
that the place we know is neither

but the way that tells us
we have been
                    not only here
but where there was the telling

it was so
            we did not choose it
it was
        so

Place

a line
colour

history
places
      never
choose
never
      it is
we know
love
    not
chosen

here

The Wayfarer

Darkness flows over the green
the horn fills with night

languid
where children are laughing

though she sings of night
she remembers
      journeys

look how thick the forest
where she has been
or where
    night
spills over

IV

Epilogue

Pictures in an Institution

1

Notice: all mirrors will be covered
the mailman is forbidden to speak
professors are confined to their offices
faculties no longer exist.

2

I speak of what I know,
how uncle Asher, spittle on his lips,
first typed with harvest hands the fox
across a fence and showing all good men
come to their country's aid rushed off to Israel
there to brutalize his wife and son

how step-grandfather Barak wiped
sour curds out of his curly beard
before he roared the Sabbath in my ears
what Sara, long his widow, dreamed
the night she cried: God, let him die at last,
thinking perhaps of Josef who had lost
jewels in Russia where the Cossack rode
but coughed his stomach out in Winnipeg

Your boredom does not matter. I take,
brutal to my thoughts, these lives, defy
your taste in metaphor; the wind-break
on the farm that Barak plowed to dust
makes images would ruin public poetry.

The rites of love I knew:
how father cheated brother, uncle, son,
and bankrupt-grocer, that we might eat
wrote doggerel verse, later took his wife,

my mother, in the English way beside my bed.
Why would he put his Jewishness aside?
Because there was no bread?
                              Or out of spite
that doctors sliced his double rupture,
fingered spleen, and healed his bowel's ache?

Lovers lie down in glades, are glad.
These, now in graves, their headstones sunk,
knew nothing of such marvels, only God, his ways,
owning no texts of Greek or anthropology.

3

Notice: the library is closed to all who read
                 any student carrying a gun
                 registers first, exempt from fines,
                 is given thirteen books per month,
                 one course in science, one in math,
                 two options
                              campus police
                 will see to co-ed's underwear

4

These names I rehearse:
                        Eva, Isaac,
Charley, Yetta, Max
                    now dead
or dying or beyond my lies

till I reeling with messages
and sick to hold again their bitter lives
put them, with shame, into my poetry.

5

Notice: there will be no further communication
                 lectures are cancelled
                 all students are expelled
                 the reading of poetry is declared a public crime

from *Life Sentence*

On the Murder of Salvador Allende

1

hopeless + remote
you peer from a balcony
your voice light as a girl's voice
                              your face
now that I look at it closely
not a pale petal   a photograph

under the flower of your face
it says here   in this unreliable
newspaper   you cried out
at last to your people

did you allow yourself
an impossible vision
                              all your countrymen
marching in rows towards guns and armour
embracing the soldiers   drowning
the colonels   with kisses and flowers

or did you
fated and tough old marxist
turn back to your desk
look again at rows of figures
                              deficits demands
the hemorrhage of capital and reserves
the streets bloody   your people defeated

2

this photograph shows a gun
silently exploding
                  there are
above the city mountains
something that looks like a man
leans out of a palace window

3

I have been taught an intricate
love of efficient death

I respond with appropriate gestures
as in this elegy
                funeral rites
for a doctor distant and unknown
my poetry itself serving the state
with its celebration of your murder

4

twice only have I met your compatriots   doctor
once in Regina a distant cousin who taught me
Neruda
        and in Toledo by the banks of the Tagus
the night sky brilliant with flowers of light
a dark boy his hands supple   singing

I know nothing of your history your people
your cause
        only a bad story about words
spoken at the coffin of your father

only this image of palaces and knives
the silent explosion of guns

it changes nothing: it goes on:
today in Omonia Square   guns in the mouth of speech

yesterday in Mozambique
                         the same taste
of death and torture
                         admirals calculating
losses and reserves

                              5

it may be   in the mines of your country
a dark face looks up briefly

in the hills remote and aloof or dully
an Indian stares at the sky

        do they remember names
        do they remember the morning of the death squad
        what stood there on the palace steps

        the morning of the death squad
        the morning of Lorca's death
        how out of bullets in his mouth poems flowered?

The Madwomen of the Plaza de Mayo

They wear white scarves and shawls.
They carry pictures on strings about their necks.
I have seen their faces elsewhere:
in Ereceira, fishermen's wives
walking in dark processions
to the sea, its roaring,
women of Ireland
wearing their dark scarves
hearing the echo of guns, bombs

Identities
the *desaparecidos*
lost ones
the disappeared

in the Plaza the Presidential Palace
reveals soldiers like fences with steel spikes
the rhythm of lost bodies
the rhythm of loss

A soldier is a man who is not a man.
A fence, a spike
A nail in somebody's eye.
Lost man.

Why are the women weeping?
For whom do they cry
under the orange moon
under the lemon moon of Buenos Aires?

"If only for humanitarian reasons
tell the families of the living
where are they
tell the families of the dead
what they need
what they deserve to know."

No one speaks.
The junta says nothing.
The *desaparecidos* remain silent.
The moon has no language.

Aguirre: Wrath of God

I will sleep with my daughter
this mad man cries and we will create
beautiful people to command
this new land which he had tried
in his madness to take from
Incas   Indians his own princes of Spain
the river itself
                    how much blood
how many shitting kings
arrowed or put to the sword

yet the truth is
few came down the river
took the breathless green
mountains
                those dark people
in their madness 137 slaughtered
thousands thousands fell before them
their book of god

so Herzog's movie moves toward its end
the mad king tottering on the raft
I reach out/touch the breasts of young women
noting the movie ends with monkeys
as if they were rats or plague
anyhow images of lust monkeys
making what we call love

Machu Picchu: by the Sacrificial Rock

There was a sickness inside me.
Bird of unknown colours.
And I thought, I will go to Peru,
to the high mountains, to the cities
Inca Lords built in impossible places.

There it will fly out of my mouth
this hissing bird. It will sound hot
as if cut from the living breast of one
held toward the sun. The Incas say,
in their bird speech, the sun is god.

And the Inca himself is a bird
who flies toward the sun.
Thousands and thousands of birds
die every day so he may be clothed
in the plumage of the sun itself.

At the stone called the sun's hitching post,
at the altar of sacrifices I waited,
the air thin as a knife blade,
my mouth opening and closing.
But the sun fell into a mist.

What is the sound of oppression
or royalty? In their markets
the Quecheuan whisper and listen,
transistors muttering to them
languages ancient and implacable.

Not even in mountains so high
they take your heart out of your mouth,
not even in cities perched like condors
where the sun rides out of the universe,
not even now will you gain or be given
ransom/release. The Quecheuan whisper
and listen, the sound of ancient bondage.

Parting at Udaipur: the Lake Palace

In Calcutta a Bengali artist explains
his family lived in a tree swarming with uncles,
incest and possession. It is an allegory.
Then there's the other story about a mongoose mother.
The tree swarms. Later his mother
will warn him she is about to die.

I think of snake charmers, how they produce
out of a sack a blur of slither
how it clamps teeth into a python's head,
savaging the dull beast.

At Gujarat an intellectual lets me know
she despises her husband, academics, poetry
her unequivocal dark hands handling a book,
poems my friend has given her.

From the Taj windows in Bombay
the Gates of India imperial and aloof
open to the Arabian sea. The heat drains
whatever leans in the wind that blows from the desert.
The harbour fills with the blood of the setting sun.

I despair of reason, knowledge, my lectures,
remember only Ann turning away at Udaipur,
the boat from the palace creating distances.
We are in a strange land. We are drifting apart.
India is between us. Across the lake, its sunken
woman, lie continents:

                    war   torture   poison
                    an apparatus of romance
                    to keep us apart.

Birds Prophesy: There Is Good, There Is Evil

This night I dream of a man with a bird's head
I have forgotten old stories about bird's prophecies:
how my mother, for example, looking at fowl
called rabbis to consult books of wisdom and law,
listened to their sayings. Birds flocking
here or there call down a rooky night.

There is no leap a man can make beyond his fate,
even if he is a bird himself,
even if he can fly beyond these vast hills.
It comes upon him like night and the cold
in high mountains carrying the death of the sun.
It comes upon him like disease on beggars.
It carries within it the substance of nightmare,
heavy wings beating inside a fearful breast,
hawk faces, vultures inside men's bodies.

Once his heart sang, once he knew bright places,
nothing was impossible, not even love itself.
He knew nothing of the birds, he knew no auguries.
He was proud. He solved riddles, knew poetry.

What will you say now to his sick heart?
What can you say of anything that soars,
even the noble bird there, beyond the sun itself?

"Grandfather's Painting": David Thauberger

Under David Thauberger's painting
showing his grandfather's house
and that giant horse standing above it,
the town of Holdfast, wheat fields,
church, elevators, and prairie grass
the TV set turned to a
Saturday Night Movie called "Marathon Man"
looks very small and peculiar,
but the movie is about politics,
betrayal and South American Nazis: it has to do
with various kinds of torture,
the use of a dentist's drill,
for example, the tyranny of McCarthy
in America of the fifties, Jews,
their memory, camps, the White Angel,
specialist in teeth, skulls, and diamonds.
      You wouldn't believe how large the horse is
in Thauberger's painting above the TV set
and yet it only portrays a symbol of how his grandfather
ruled the land, the power by which the little town
was run, the motor of the little town called Holdfast
while beneath it the real powers that run us,
pictures, say, and how we know how to kill one another,
metaphors of murder, these are played out night
upon night and I watch them and watch the painting,
no longer knowing whether I should write poetry,
especially poems about land, about Estevan,
or about why I came back to Regina, Saskatchewan,
this cold winter of 1979 or what I thought
I might find in a city of this kind to write of,
now that my father is dead for many years, and my mother,
and most of my friends are in the arts.
                                        There are nights
cold enough to kill. They remind me of my boyhood,
how much I loved the winter on the prairies, never
believing it was deadly or that we fought to be alive here
though my fantasies were of war. That powerful animal,
this evening with the Marathon Man running,
running, I suddenly know David was right to paint him,

his grandfather. We stand over the land, fathers,
and over our homes and over each other.
We have terrible forces inside us: we can paint them,
green, acrylic, glitter: the form never lies.
The truth is in the long dead winters where we live.

In My 57th Year

This is the year my mother lay dying
knocked down by tiny strokes she claimed
never once hit her though when she lay
crib-like where they laid her there she wept
for shame to be confined so near her death.
This is the year the cancer inside my father's
groin began its growth to knock him down
strong as he was beside his stricken wife.
This is the year I grew, ignorant of politics,
specious with law, careless of poetry.
There were no graves. The prairie rolled on
as if it were the sea. Today my children make
their way alone across those waves.
Do lines between us end as sharply
as lines our artists draw upon the plains?
I cry out. They keep their eye upon
their politics, their myths,
careful of lives as I was careless.

What shall I say? It is too late to tell again
tales we never knew. The legends of ourselves
spill into silence. All we never said, father
to daughter, son to unmanned man, we cannot say
to count the years.
                    I no longer know time or age
thinking of parents, their time, their grave of names.
Telling the time, fiction consumes me.

UNPUBLISHED, UNCOLLECTED POEMS

The Abstract Man

The abstract man in his rage
removed his arms and legs,
undid the buttons of his chest,
unzipped his final chord,
to find the music box within.

Alas, inside the abstract man
only circles of desire swam
upon an oily lake of rainbows,
an odoured marsh of spectrums.

Apothecary, sweeten him.
Is there no drug for motion
or for lust to fasten him,
to hook him from his lake?
Where is the king or magi
who will mend the unzipped
disappointed abstract man?

Accident

Where points meet in the snow
Many matters are finally determined;
Pleased with our free speed
We rush to liberty through snow.

For speed composes us; heart beats
And things race through the blood;
Our subject is our living as we go
Over the veins where the fast blood heats.

Collisions release us and we are free
And rusting hulks handle this weather
Objectively, that yesterday
Shone as they sped now melt or freeze,
There is no other.

We are become things, and only
The blood runs now where it is free
And spelled in red headlines
Over the girl's lips and loins
That free fluid goes;
Nor can she pull herself together
Where she lies in the snow,
Nor any anti-freeze keep her from cold.

Alice in Daliworld

Burned in his wonderland by the Possible Man
He was left ashes at the foot of a sphinx
Of his own devising and a puzzle
He had cooked up in his own embers.

He remained there weeping, the unphilosopher,
Tail end of a Cheshire cat which had
Ceased to smile, he was its disappeared remainder;
And tried with all the rhymes he'd ever heard
To please it into coming back again.

As one by one the skulls of his endeavour fell
He stepped across them and he tried again
Until the sphinx and all the clocks had flown away.

Then, legendary hero in his Daliworld,
He flew about encountering Queens
And courtezans, and Kings who lavished gold
On him who was a favorite until morning
And his own impossible self marched by:
O see its head of snakes and eyes
Grow great and weep to find him stone.

The Anatomy of Marriage

An Epithalamium

Consubstantiality, as much as blood,
The chemistry thereof seeks to bind her to me;
As when two swans struck white by sun,
Sinless as galleons, go sailing
Down that sweet river to its end.

O feel of dovesoft palms, O hands
That beg from touch a sacrament
Asking ungiveable alms;
Religious arms, O impossible lips,
When body, learning, will you know,
In this lachrymose dusk,
The only sign you will be given
Is the natural fission,
The religiosity of seem?

Ancestral Voices Prophesying War

Voice of an Old Man:

These lands inhabited by tribes
Rich with the bones of bison, bulge
Every spring, wheat shoots shine
In the green sun, gulleys gush
Water, and gulls hover over the land
Seeing the ocean. Birds see far.
They are omens. Watch for the high
And haughty hawk. See where he halts
On the air and drops, heavier than rain,
There the rodent runs. Beware of rats,
Weasels, badgers. When the doe runs
That is a rich spring and bushes bear fruit.
Count the numbers in the lead flock.
I have seen many springs. There are gods
In the land. Listen. The herd moves
Always together and strays fall.

Voice of a Young Man:

Mutterings of god in an old man's brain.
Geometrical and spare, the ice-hard lines
Are clear and still as frost, a metaphor
Of silence. My image is the water
On the still lake, hard as silver.
The word is pitch and pay, and oaths
As hard as clay, baked in the sun,
Fall on the prairie. It is a dray-horse
Of a land, all tendon and the froth
Of bitten steel upon its mouth.
See on its flanks the hard blue scars
Of time, the whip, and welts of dusty green.
See where the river sinks into the land.

Voice of a Woman:

Why are you making poems?
There are such things to be done.
Already it is spring, the flies buzz
By the oven, in the fields the land bakes,

Loaves quicken, and at night the moon is thin.
What priests are you to take the young
Into the fields at night and set them
Quarreling in their blood with voices
Of the wind, the trees, the river?
Where is my child? To which new tree
Nailed now?

Animals, Gods and Wise Men

Animals, gods and wise men
     and women who branch out like trees
   in great showers of words
     or whose feet are roots
  or who sway from the thighs like boughs
     or saplings in a wind

animals, gods and wise men
     and a forest of women in the spring
  whose thighs are like young trees
     bare of the gnarled bark of years
  or the knots of rings
  hooping the finger like a knuckled clock
     in the chronicle of spring

swaying around the pool
    the naked trees their arms
    embracing air their obscene roots
    the ground around the pool
    where weary in the heat of time
    the sweaty carter and his horse
      lie down and down beside them
  in the shade of boughs lie down
     animals, gods and wise men.

and limbs sweat: from her thighs
      a wise old naked tree sweats
cooling juices
    in the stream lie down to bathe
    their muscles knotted in the sweat of time
    animals, gods and wise men

Anna Dromeda

" Of remedies of love she knew per chaunce
For she koulde of that art the olde daunce."

Yon silly bird stretching in the queer Aprille twilight
Stares for a while, hath foreboding of shadows;
Folds ancient neck and head beneath a wing
As the green world goes under and the night-
Time is icumen in…

Lhude sings the owle

The wife puts up her hair in curls
While tapping her Sweet Cap against the tray
Examines teeth in her bright mirror, coils
Downward in an arc to pare a corn
With expert razor claws, inspects
Her nostrils, scratches at a thigh,
Unfolds the pillowcase, retires with a sigh.

Lady we are for the dark

Oh Harry you were king and promised me the world

The gentle cockroach, nervous arrow, slides
And scrapes in cracks along the wall;
Susie and Allan
Whisper in the hall

And here another faded soul goes by
With clawed feet trickling on the floor
While soute stars hath shone in darkness o'er
The moths that flit and totter on the glass
And night of stars and insects populate the grass.

Sweet girl (whose gat teeth scarce deplore
Thy budding mouth) Sweet girl
How wearily I lay me down by thee

Oh sweet king Harry night comes on

Enthroned in darkness wife she lay
With fairest Harolde by her side.
Encased in armour, he, the insect king
Went scuttling over mountains for his bride
Of twenty days, chattering like the cricket,
Bold was his boast for Anna, whom he'd free
With winged heels and countenance
That shineth as the aspect of the sea,
Full fair. With sails set to the north
The hero Harolde, childe of Rolande,
Mixed up his metaphors
And tottered forth.

Pearl nebulae, ring of stars,
Constellation of night enfolding my love and I;
Anna Dromeda lies in her bed and stares
At the stars with an acquisitive eye
And sings in her chains like the sea.

Anxiety

Kierkegaard & Heidegger:
      in the finger-nail file
    a tooth gleams
northern pike slip the weeds
and the mountain nods

out of the window a pail leans
    the water yellow in the sun
       shark in the prose
     takes chunks
of the clambering bather

at the councilman's dance
   three spilled sentences
   lay in their stained syntax
     ashen words

the burning language reds the sea

Arendt's *Eichmann in Jerusalem*

Hannah, my dear, do you hear how your voice has changed?
    Your tonsils at night now speak by themselves
    like false teeth clacking in a glass
    like the limbs of an amputee
    rattling about his room
    while he dreams of full-bodied maidens
    twirling their thighs around his astonished sex

    voice of the locust
    bearded woman's voice
    voice of the camp castrati
    scratchy pen's voice
    blue voice in the rubber stamp
    voice of the squeaking condom urging death
    voice of the bidet
    the sound of the journalist's flushing, flushing

Hannah, where are your woman's tears that should have
    turned my *New Yorker* to pulp
    and turned to pulp the letters in the bag
    so that my Eaton's Account cried out
    so that Calgary Power turned green with grief
    so that the Jasper Sewer vomited red sorrow
    so that, Hannah, letters showered upon me
    a huge alphabet of limbs, eyes, teeth,
    so that the letters of your grief spelled out
    your grief

"for politics is not like the nursery"
nor is it a womb
nor is it an entrance nor an exit
nor the singing of Miriam on the shore
nor the cry of Klein in the second Gloss
nor is it a woman's voice
or a nipple
or the embracing limb
the wheeling world
the moon-lapping tide

Do you love him that you use his mouth
who should have sung how waters choked a king
and how before the lepers fell on you, clean limbed,
we counted Pharaoh's dead beside the bloody shores?

Argument

For the critic it was always plain sailing.
With a full wind his two master plunged ahead
And like the Pequod in the halcyon days
It was whaling whaling all the way.

But they never saw that snow-hill-white whale.
The wind was always right and fair.
More equators than Mercator dreamed of were crossed
And more stars than Copernicus dreamed of
Went by the dangerous swaying mast.

And all the while in the murderous rooms
At Twickenham and Strawberry Hill and Horton
And by that terrible table in the Mermaid Tavern
The poets kept talking and scratching out lines
More wicked than the undulating Cephalopod.

The first gleeman mouthing a ribald song
In that rollicking language played for a coin
And was thought less trouble than heroes.
And never he nor all the crowd knew
What a quarrel they had started in Webster's brain
Who, for example, would put Tourneur and Milton
In the same beer parlour to share a pint?

At Lidice

His blood flowed with theirs
   bestowing grace

Blond dumb open broad
    stubborn   German   face
Afraid

Left alone
Left until last
Asking nothing
Demanding nothing
Promising nothing
Receiving nothing

knowing and unknowing
alive and dead
dead and alive

A Christ died on Calvary
A man died at Lidice
   knowing and unknowing

His blood flowing with ours
   bestowing grace

(In 1942, as a reprisal for the assassination of Heydrich,
the Nazis destroyed "forever" the town of Lidice, popula-
tion 700, by killing all the men, and deporting all the
women and children and razing all the buildings. There is a
legend that one German soldier refused to obey the order
to shoot. He was warned that he himself would be shot
unless he complied. He again refused and was murdered.)

The Axe-Murder Poems

*"Lizzie Borden took an axe
Gave her mother forty wacks"*

it was after all a resolution
    each time I struck her I knew
how to separate flesh from idea

    this isnt the right language
    to find her body her head
    to understand

The Night of the Axe Murders

axe-murder poems become possibilities
    the question remains technical
how to write
        whether precise
    knowledge should be part
    what kinds of axe to use
    where the blow is either more
    or less painful

I begin to consider possibilities

The Bach Preludes and Fugues

I

48 times he said this
which is 48 times the
elementary joy

those exercising hands
say
    lifted toward
    the tent's peak
    where the flags
    lag in listless
    circles
        over and over
he says what he says
this equals that
    moon (say)
    crying
    about sun
    equals
        sun
    crying
    about moon

or so, sometimes,
death is life
this rag-a-bag
woman
    kettle
    and pot
elementary joy
of knowing
the 48 deaths
are the 48 lives

657

II

I have gone at evening
among the tents of his music
seeing his clowns tumbling
in their circular pants
I have gone from his cinema
to his sculpture to his 48
pieces of 48 pieces
asking myself
about all that Israel
panting for its Samson
who found the dog-God
barking in the clowning God

III

Look, if my fingers could hold,
Before they fell from me, my roots,
My budding hands, the plums of summer,
The summer plums like eyes, like cars
Or car lights, purple, in the summer sun,
The flowering fingers of my hands
And the shabby 48 times my leafy hands
Let fall the summer from my hands
Do you think I would say this equals
Simply that, this moon, say, equals
Simply the summer sun, this pot
And these kettles equal simply

I would rather in our tents
He spoke to me of his father
And why he wanted to sing
Why he thought it was God to die
Or even to go back to that valley
Where the young bones shone
And the bright mules bled
Before the flowering plums
Before the final flowering sun.

Beach at Miraflores

From the high cliffs above Miraflores
Lima offers among its slovenly streets
Far from favellas festering like mud houses
a Boschian hell, its own demonology.
Consider the garbage of the rich
or at least the middle class, those with dogs
on their roofs, guardian shepherds of rich
Lebensroom: here the mess comes down
plastics, cardboard, condoms to the rhythm
of the sea it will wash out on Pacific tides
the mess, it will dissolve there in the mild
seas like the blood of the Incas, like the mud cities
that the Chimus built, like their gold labyrinths.

Here in the Regina library far beyond the gold,
the madness that the sun drove into Spanish minds
I hear an endless drone: this one learning languages,
that one grammar, that one how to read.
In Peru I thought I know these words:
put down the list of those taken by Conquistadors
to rooms of torture or those the Inquisition took
to pieces bone by tendoned bone. The prairie night
grows deadlier in its cold. I listen to the dark
come on, words drifting like garbage from the cliffs
of Lima, poisoned city: "I wonder what lies ahead."
So little to say. So little to learn.
Only the deaths of the inevitable story.

The Beauty of Pure Act as the Final Cause

1

Act

beside a pillar
               a torn dress

in a pool of light
               a blunt spear
               tipped with hair

like this sun porch
               the hottest sun
is watered by the evening light

2

Pure Act

the blind window sees the widow
in her act
         winnowing the spear

she steps into a pool of light
         scatters the sun's grain

3

Final Cause

a bird breaks loose from a stone
the bird-faced lady like a tree
shudders in a splurge of light

she spills a pearl upon my porch.

Betrayal Beginning in Dreams

To the memory of Delmore Schwartz

let muzhik assure you   volk
when those seven silk consonants
tangled around the heart
of one ruptured vowel
half down in the elevator
of the columbia hotel in new york city
and the great rabbit fell
against all the buttons
including *emergency*   and *open*
he saw it all then
clearer than a honed diamond
that if
in dreams begin responsibilities
and we are all sometimes icons
though certainly not a movie
then one's life ends with
betrayal beginning in dreams

ah volk
if dreams were only a wolf
that knows the pissedbleached coordinates
of its boundaries
if all games
            were as simple
            as a young boy
            in the evening grass
            he murmuring to a young girl
            trembling in fear where
            the sun stains
            her thin
                        thigh

    "don't cry... let me inside you
    i will stop the bleeding"

if myth were as simple
as the two drunken brothers
who reportedly
               threw the bride from the *troika*
               to pursuing wolves

if magic were as simple
as the left hand flashing out to encompass
the fly
the captor a granite stare straight ahead
if betrayal were as simple
as wind rising
when the tightrope walker
reaches halfway
if it were all as simple
as the first glimmerings in the left eye
of your dearest friend
who lighting your wife's cigarette
after love
as they sit up when you are out of town
thinks
i know so much
...about him now
the trick...not to get caught
getting away with it
a kind of magic!

if the heart's hattrick
were all this simple
there would be nothing   volk
nothing
          to worry about
          or suffer in the clarity of things
          during insomnia

but we secretly know   volk
it's all myth
and words
          muzhik believing only
          in a world of real people
          and those who know
          the smell of earth
          just after a rain

and a place
where one is born first
and named later

do you remember   volk
the story muzhik told us?
the nameless woman from illinois
once raped and beaten
along a rural road during the depression
the woman who forgot her name
during multiple shock treatments
to calm her
in various insane asylums
and was finally transferred
to a nursing home
where mrs shroud recalled

> "She wouldn't let men near her.
> She was terrified of men.
> She shook constantly from 50
> years of medication, but appeared
> to enjoy her new freedom
> from mental institutions,
> wearing a ragged pink sweater
> as she walked around the
> nursing home even in rainstorms."

she died last year
at 71   and yesterday
the state of illinois
buried a nameless urn
                    of ashes
that's the *real* world
going about its own business
volk   the imagination
doesn't stand a chance!

volk   we know the realities
that while our mothers walked the margins
of those dark forests
in an old country
from *selo*   to *selo*
                    to work

wolves' smouldering eyes moving
in the shadow of fear
didn't smoulder for woman
but only for the ruffian
and his sordid companions
who believed there was something
to get away with

and yes volk
that prairie magician's line
that always fascinated us so much

> "now folks   jis watch real close
> cause yeh know the hand's
> faster than the eye—that's why
> yeh see so many black eyes
> hee hee hee!"

the line was pure bullshit!
a myth from the american west
the fastest hand
a myth that became an earwig
crawling into the ear
and boring into the brain
of a sleeping gunman
who wakened to become golem's automaton
volk   we know *the fastest hand*
is nothing at all
nothing
and that the magic beyond all magic
deals not in cards
but in the perfect magic of words
and linguistic tricks
where humour can make people laugh so hard
they cry
as the magician guest
vanishes
    with the finest
    oriental vase
    casually tucked
        in his pocket

muzhik!   you're joshing me now!
try it volk
try it anytime   anywhere
it works everytime
you can steal crystal wine glasses this way
the finest silver is yours
i've even seen them exit
with a friend's wife

but if muzhik can return for a moment
to *serious* matters   volk
you know that friendship is at least
as fragile as glass
and that anyone can form a fist
in mercurial rage
and turn a picture window
into a spider web
during that split second
of impact
        the left   or right hand
        do the job
        equally well
        but it takes something else
        another kind of person
        and voice
        to sustain a single note
        powerful enough
        to shatter glass

the trick of all tricks   volk
is not what the man in darkness
that makes him you
speaks
in the fear of discovery
      but the poem's hattrick
      on the margins
      of betrayal
      guilt
      and responsibility to dreams
      where a single
            misplaced word
      can break
            the heart

Cabbages and Trees

The peculiarities of death
   and its extravagance
like a shopkeeper's manual
are not what I had bargained for

are not the steadiness of breath,
   my heart's acceptable dance.

I thought perennial not annual
   trees were planted here
     were what we grew
but death has branches too.

Chair

For P.S.

We moved into the airless space
Between the table and the chair.
While standing there with all the grace
Of footmen, who with livery wear
The faceless air of vacant space,

We wondered if the ouija board
Would help us hear, or help us see,
The levitating table scored
And humbled with the knocking knee.
"Yes," we said; "No," said the board.

We turned from magic, where the wall
Held all the algebra of air,
Back to the geometric hall,
Which led us from the cushioned chair
To day, and there there was no wall.

      "Maybe," said the table,
      "Maybe you are able."
      "Never," said the chair,
      "You would never dare."
      But the airless space,
      From an aching void,
      Only made a face:
      And that we enjoyed.

Chelydra Serpentina

Ironic in his house of bone
this turtle hoists a skeleton
one hundred years or more in mud
always the ice of hate his blood
cousin in name to singing dove
without that turtle's house of love
the naked serpent in the bone
Ironic in his house of stone

Cold Pastorals

When I scorned the new architecture
    (refused to pray at its masses)

and when in the understandable ground
    a silver tree blossomed

I saw that my companions
    were truly Norwegian
    fiercer than walrus.

Over the land where they ran
    Welsh villages crumbled
    and stones were flung
    into the Druidical sun.

You will say the lass
    whom we buried in Norway
    never existed
No architects mass
    buried her. No one shrieked.

But when the Norwegians run
    and when there is again
    a silver tree, in the day
    dying, she will walk on
    no print shown,
    a white, simple lawn.

The Criminal Element

In the ecclesiastical night
   robed like a bishop
   or a wizard
         not even grasshoppers awake
somewhere a saint unrobed herself
bathed from a dipper, came out fire
as though she contained stars.

I rubbed myself awake
       no longer congregational
       myself unorbited about hymns
       fled into the startling planet
       called by no universal name.

Compatriots in pity
in the chains of office
sang official anthems.

       No one understood
       no one knew
       no one heard
the other song, ancient as fire
when the last mayor but one
went Indian and scalped his councillors,
three secretaries, and the incumbent
elected by the reform administration,
whose motto (under God) was:
     "Time for a change
     clean government
     sewers for every home
     Time for a change."

The Dark Chapel

someway into the wilderness
    north of Estevan
    on route 39
        contemptuous of meaning
        left behind
        with the orators
        with the parliamentarians
only the highway now
a ribbon, a snake
        whatever the critics say
        since there was no choice
        never any real choice
only the town suddenly behind
        despicable, squat,
        a huddle of shacks
and the king murmuring about harps,
evil angels, quoting Browning's
Childe Roland or acting like Saul
in the caves, in the dark valley
the Souris, mean source,
river of frogs
        a croaked song
Ezra says,
        sunset and grasshoppers flying

What will you do then with the road
down which the memorable dead
travel like crooked fathers?
Humped in the valley, fathers,
who avoided politics
who gained the crooked image

The Daze of Men like Suns

When vanity superbly finishes the sea,
As silent as the sun retracts its gaze,
Our eyes bereaved no longer cling, without
That ancient prodigal, our infancy.

When we are done, both lip and eyebrow spent,
Mouth clasped, the dusk evolved about,
(It is not long and you will cry to go)
Think how the silent other went…

Gone to the sea, our prodigal, plunged
Silent in the salt, a red rage broke his brain.
He gazed too long, went blind withal
And left a bright confession of his pain.

Well think how marygold the summer waits.
Console his service with a gorgeous love like lips.
"What sets today will rise tomorrow."
Only the silent sea returns and laps

Up to the night… the waves will bind the glare
And turn the vain and smirking sea about;
Tides wash a fabled shadow back and forth
And from it, only murder will come out.

Not suns, the sea gives back, that took the waves,
Broke, went beneath; only the drowned man's bones,
Death's bounty, blood on sand will lie,
A scattered alphabet which no one owns.

The Death of the Morning

he remembered sunlight

> The golden shower must have been like rain,
> For when a world is bathed in such a light
> The eye is blind. It seems as if the brain
> Is touched by the feel of things in its own right.

he remembered sunlight on a wall

> The texture of things is more than in the mind;
> The fire burns forever on the sand;
> When flame no longer is, it burns behind
> The optic nerve, beyond the feeling hand.

he remembered a wall near a street

> Down in the dung a pigeon flutters,
> Ruffling his feathers under the rain,
> And scratching for seed in the sand.

he remembered a street to a river

> The water is running away in the gutters;
> The wind is blowing about in the brain;
> St. Elmo bathes the lifted hand.

he remembered river, street and wall
he remembered sunlight
he remembered nothing at all

A Dialogue of the Body and the Soul

Body: Good light, my friend, I am for the dark
Where, save a dream, imitating death
I'll sleep this night away from you.

Soul: And yet there is the sea of sleep within your eyes,
Who knows what fish you'll find when you have left
And lost this shore of senses? Now you'll sail
From ghost to ghost within your left and lost past.
Happy voyage—and surprise.

Body: Avoid the moral; stay, and hear the lightfall
Now it's filled with stirs.

Soul: That's eve's ring you hear.
From nightchime through moonday a wedding of the sun
And moon has filled the air with song
From house to hilltip, school to skill, top to toe

Body: And desk to doom.

Soul: A clown from your red birth
To your black death, all mouth and motion;
Peristalsis and paralysis, the twin pillars
Of your creation and redemption; a muscle
Twitching through eternity...

Body: Leave off,
Eternity? Your holy day has failed,
Each comes at last to its weak end,
A day of haplessness, a sun day
Gone into night from nurse to bed.

Soul: It's so within the circle that you please
To travel in, a five-laned highway of the senses,
Why think that you have seen the mind's whole country?

Body: I see what is to be seen. At night
I only want to rest; the rest is silence,
Save a dream.

Soul: Which I save for you.
Arterial roads to the heart of a city,
A vain way when I am winged, and fury
Is the flight and free…

Body: Icarus?

Soul: Yes, and not the Minotaur. You pace
From cell to cell, bolted by bones;
Your own prison and the mind-forged manacles
I see upon you. You have no spirit
Or you would be free. You have no spirit
Except me.

Body: I have a nose for non-sense though.

Soul: Yes, and your world smells for it too.
To be hung in cartilage, framed in flesh,
And stuck between two jellies ringed with hair
And sticky with old tears for griefs I name,
To be dragged down into mankind…

Body: Now wait. What keeps you upright? Being
Fastened to my feet. I am a cliff you hang upon,
Don't push me or you'll fall. And think on this:
For me, the horizontal man, love
Is always vertical and I must stoop to it.

Soul: Play all those angles, make a cross, but think on this:
Your sodden heart, soaked in its own blood, and beating
Like a drum thuds in my ears too. I'm deaf with it.
I'm blinded with your eyes.

Body: Now who's at sea?
Give over, for I'll never rest. It is enough
That day by die I must trip forward
And must always make me from what's always at my back
And that I'm never what I'll be but what I was.
Where's thought for that? Take all the time you want,
But let me rest.

Soul: Poor spectre time,
          The haunt of those who watched him. Turn your back on him
          And see he isn't there.

Body: And lose myself?
          I'd rather have him, bones and all,
          Than be a ghost myself. We shouldn't have named him.
          Look, the night is pale and tired. Doom is almost here.
          The bird of yawning now it seems has flown.

Soul: Night after light and you'll be deaf and blind and dumb
          Through noons of sun for all the pasts to come.

Body: Night into day and day becoming light.
          Good light, good friend, good light.

Soul: Good die, you mean, the doom is almost here.
          Good die, my friend, till dawnsdays reappear.

Body: Good die, my friend, till life do us part.

Soul: Good die.

Body: Good die.

Edmonton's Streets Are Numbered

8400-15000
                    is a street
I have no story of
                    no way
this street becomes god
                    or god's way
(I mean destruction's way
or a slough, the sun sunk,
the pool a hive of eyes
                    I mean
despair on the street
in the narrow way
the people shrunk
                    small as a fist
                    faces like fists
and muscles wound
all over their thin bones
like vines around trees
or ropes of greed
I once saw a tailor sew
for a town of friends
who put a kettle on my head)

                    unstoried street
winds into (no) destruction
                    (no) grief
            (no) kettle of
                    fried-
            (the shrunk fish, dead
            three days lay on the murky
            sun-left sand-stuck lively
            with flies shore
                    deft with death

    I could not swallow)

only the snow, white explosion,
kills for my daughter
                    fishful of summer

                    and the unstoried houses
a fistful
                    a cat sniffs
a whole summer of fish
whose skeleton lies
                    a tin (awry)
                              kettle

Epitaph

These removed from context are
The unpunishable dead
Their meaning is
Not a glory from afar

Now unambiguous they lay
Like headstones heads away

And they are ungrammatical
A few confusions
What their pursed lips say
Is said
And is not glory

Oh they are far from language
Though they lie
In our best poetry

Now unambiguous they lay
Like headstones heads away

Experiment with Arabesque, Attar of Roses, and Shaving Lotion

One saint I've seen
who could walk on water.

He was bug-eyed and bow-legged.

Antic and nimble
He disposed me to worship,
A contortion
that threw my limbs
Into exceptional joints
Among other bugs.

I still limp on feast days,
stare long at filmy pools,
am wary of boots and fishermen.

Often I dream of drowning.

And sometimes think
a rotting fruit
has lodged in my side.

* * *

the bard within me keeps his peace

exotic in attar the pink frail
dangles pails of rings
I expect never to sing again
some of my friends dream of spit
others of a far country

look how the teasle and the water bug
scatter the elements, one walks
like a bow-legged saint over the waves
shall I worship him

cataracts of cumulus are nimble northward
but the air, my lord, weighs on me
like a blue goose-feather quilt
and the traffic streams like a storm
down gulleys of liquid tar

whom shall I praise
when the bulldozer jack-knifes the trailer
when the bug-eyed cars bulge and burst
and out of wrenched doors stream
the innards

Sinbad slew a heart in a tower
nembutal purpled the face of a ponce

* * *

I walk along the loam and clay
most of my friends have chastised me
toward the north the land is grey
the word is immorality

capricious cumulus is nimble where
three friends spoke solemnly
over the blue goose-feather air
the word is immorality

look where the teasle and the water bugs
scatter the elements, I say,
my friends are solemn in their rags
the word is immorality

one bug-eyed bow-legged saint
walks the waves incessantly
endless is my friends' complaint
the word is immorality

exotic in attar one pink frail
dangles his rings, his finery…

Expostulation and Reply

Unto my enmity give cause, your Honour
While lawyer-like I powder hair and curls,
Adjust my passions on my robe
And wear my conscience as a wig of morals.

1

Remembering man in the hooked net struggling like fish,
Fin and frantic body lashing the roped cruel skein;
Or in a stupor, stunned and desolate, lying upon the deck,
With a last desultory lunge slipping from freedom

Where in the long wet sea was to be free and wet
For the shark's mouth and the black coiled squib
And the sucking arms; between fisherman and fury
Caught, suspended between sea and air, not amphibious;

Who desired to fly and scarcely yet could swim;
Remembering man like salmon in a massed pack
All alive amid the slapping of body to body,

Would you be elite, clean, singing to flowers, marvellous,
Innocent, darling sheep-herder, flock tender,
Watching for stars and the straining hymn on the meadow;

Or be film-eyed, staring, flopping among others, fish,
While framed in flesh song gropes from gaping mouth?

Now must mind not only delight with aspect of war,
Denuded and not virgin proceed to arms;
But certainly no longer laughing among lambs
Be a horticulturalist or lover of flowers

Or with a long and crooked stave guide herds,
Or being herded, in the huddled warmth delight.

For a fever comes on and in the sick silver rising
Of thermometer, traces the quarrel of blood
The muttering worry of pulse

Where vision comes only to the staring eye
Bloodshot from gazing too long at the sun
Or those whitened and turned inward to the fretful mind
Where birds go with their delicate innocent feet

And where grows the moist foetus uncurling
To push from love, fish, ape to mind and man
Is that strained song, more important than murder,
Than the bleeding of man, than liberation,
Almost more important than the poet himself.

Fable

Beyond the city's wreck, we reached the plains.
Everything will be all right now, I was told.
There is nothing to fear. The way
Lies northward till you reach the cold.

The Mayor and his Councillors, rolled
In parkas of the finest fur you'd find
South of the fur belt, a sort of rabbit,
Hurried past me, teeth bare in the wind.
I cried after them, but one said, Never mind,
You know we cant stop here,
We have the mines upon our list today.

They dwindled into balls of fur
And later, hopping back, in a rage of fear
They hurried past me, crying: Please beware
The Caribou, They're moving south in herds.
It wasnt Caribou. It was birds.

Flocks came out of the north
Like a convention of Episcopalian
Ministers, all black with white bands
Around their throats, and they called to me,
The gold, the gold.

I thought perhaps they meant go south.
After all, perhaps there the green goat,
With his wineskin, leaps in the garden.
But I was wrong.

For they were childish birds,
Their thin collars clutched about their throats,
I heard them shrieking in small voices:
The Mayor and his Ministers cant be wrong.
And I knew the way was northward, and the end
Just as it had been foretold.

Fairy Tale

common miss jennifer dreaming in the gold sun-
light, flaxen miss jennifer with her coiledyellow hair;
two bumpy palms turned up begging for a prince
miss jennifer dreams in the goldsun

and twelve strong years put arms around her
rubbed fire in her thighs and with a splash
went like a goldfish, left a mist in her eyes
those pale wet blue eyes

well fortunately she never knew prince george
grimy george with his muscular legs
who tupped seven girls and rubbed his hairy palms
and gave them silver for alms.

Fake

I think of you
practicing his signature
imitating his voice
that scrambled syntax

maybe one night
the thought comes furiously
he is writing your autobiography

on that truth
the Republic itself founders
and my dominion

Art   after all
                    denies us
knowing
                    prisons (prove) real

The Familiar Wakening

you wake again to the familiar dark
and the meticulous survey begins:
tax accounts in numbers you couldnt dream of
lectures whose structure defies your memory
in the sodden coasts of your bed
you lie streaming with guilt

Fear and Trembling

Innocent faces are not innocent
And the simple eye reveals
The signal glance, the signal sent
Confirming witnesses' intent.
Into the corners where extend
Ends of the interlocking web
The insect hand of law explores,
Exploring shakes the centre, where,
Bearded and golden as the sun,
Crouches the cancerous spider.

Flood Scene

Night long the poor were praying in the house
That wept and sank its timbers in this sand
The intermittent sound of prayer rose on the land
Like waves collapsing into sand

Arcless, the lapse was present in their sinking eyes:
Old sockets, shocked by loss, flared only once
Before collapsing into blackened rims of ruin
The town and all the people wavered in the flood

Sunk here, below, above the waves, I hear
The whispers coming up, watered and shoaled,
Like shells rimming a total history of bone

Over the total waste as once before
Now see the basket sky append
An egg below to hatch each morning
Morning's opening and end
Gold wickered in a pompous cage
An age of luminosity, a light that's dying
All light's lying here.

From "The Memoirs of a Public Accountant"

You see then to what we have come. The street angles and tilts,
  houses dangling now over the edge of a chasm while
  within the earthquaking town the casual stranger tilts
  his hat and the sun, his hair pleasant and yellow as wheat,
  draws himself into a child's serene face. What are we to
  make of such contradictions? I have a daughter who sings
  and who runs, who takes the sun in her hands and tosses it
  like a ball over the side of my house and catches the moon
  on the other side and tosses it back to the other side, and
  a son who drives giant animals to his will and with his palms
  slays enormous machines and eats various-coloured people.
You would be surprised to know what words I have not said to my
  colleagues, and how many times I have stood shivering before
  a storm that did not happen, the thunderous strokes of a pen
  shaking the floor. Of course, nothing of this is in any way
  an excuse or an offering. Too terrible to contemplate what
  I have already given to the insatiable officers. How else
  can I explain? There were the sailors. If I admitted that?
  Or told everything about the women? Or noted even more carefully
  what the lecturer was saying, transcribing every word in my
  notebook? Nothing will do now except to admit what cannot be said.
  The day is already gone and I walk toward the gates which will
  shut only once.
      I refuse to blame the others.
      I refuse to blame myself.
      I refuse to accept the official explanation.
      I refuse to blame the children.
Nothing more is possible except to refuse, the forming word unsaid
  and unspeakable the speechless image that will fall like fire
  upon the very gates when the furnace itself at the end comes
  up to be the crown.

A Fragment

And silently the streets stalked after me
And I was small and grey beneath their stare,
Sorrow sped down and burst the veil of air
And shadows leaped, and swallows fled from me.

And did the night sing once, then die
As bolts of flame raced over futile blue
And was the world a chorus too
And what did sudden voices there imply?
-
Blinded, the moon fell from the sky
Tall buildings stood, then rushed apart
And secret to the dark's unerring eye
A blasphemy unveiled its heart.

Published in *The Students' Standard*, 30 March, 1946

A Fragment

Dark girl, whom I lay lately down beside,
Who was the material of fleeing flame
The unexpected bright guardian of the substance of day,
In whose eyes, in whose dusty glance, fallen to the ground
Lay, as the moon lay, a sleeping allegory...

And there are roses the color of blood,
There are flowers that must have wept petals
And dawn dew at the absence of night

Though I have been mapping ceaselessly
Such terrain, whitening the unexplored country:
While she is the color of rose
She is a black rose...

Look into my eyes that have cried
Because time wastes with scorn
A black rose.

A Gloss of Poems

(Remembering Abe Klein)

1

Break down the twigs, break down the boughs
But break not, Lord, the golden bowl.

(A.K.)

My body is tree
my reaching boughs and twigs
are skeleton
meant to be
broken by stone
by shouldering snow
splintered by rain
cracked by the fingering frost

My body is given, Lord
to show Thy ways
I read where my roots go
assess the green
count leaves' ascension
into heaven's blaze

This will I willingly
submit to Thee:
my skeleton,
my tree.

2

And lives alone, and in his secret shines
like phosphorous. At the bottom of the sea.

(A.K.)

Drowned? Were you the one
drowned
or do I dream again
and do I hold again your hand across a table
in a Chinese restaurant
hand reaching to affirm
against the goyem laughter?

A drowned man now... Your hand
that delicate instrument
long servant to
the fervent ferment of thought
your hand lies twitching out
a spider's mark
on the bare table

And in the hive, your head
the golden bowl,
bees buzz and bumble
fumble for honey amidst empty cells
where the slain poems
wingless, tremble.

A Gothic Tale

I watched them for an afternoon
that simple Greek and stubborn monk
   under the market-hunting sun
   under the cul-de-sac, the moon.

You would not think a clown in brown,
   a monk of fashion, townish monk,
   gloved in the cloth of Orient,
   modish in lamb of Asian mode

could fence that simple Greek around
   with blatant fashion, point of lace,
   such is the pride of market-place,
   such is the monkish pride of play.

The lance that tumbled him to mud,
   O wicked lance, O fashioned play,
broke Thebes, shook Greece, sprayed
pigeon feathers red with pigeon blood

over a jovial sky and cracked the pate
   of heaven like an egg, with lance
   as sharp as steeple, then it put
my Grecian knight into the bloody mud.

Well, who will protect us now
   from sights that we must see?
Truth has its fashions in the market-place
ladies will wear this monkish lace

but Lady Moon is cracked by fashion
   and I may grieve for her
she was whiter by far than any monk
   and easy with her favours.

The Head of Orpheus
Floating Upon the River Hebrus
Speaks This:

It is, of course, the chance missed,
But more, remembering why it was done.
On the voyage no one was annoyed
While I was singing. It was good enough
Then to make songs about trees
Who were lovely women, about the winds
Who were old men, and a god in the sky.
After they had the fleece, they became
Different somehow. Music wasn't enough.

It is the chance missed, you have no way
Of knowing this, not at the time, not when
The scroll is handed you, the judges
In their robes of black brocade look down
Expectantly, the crowd is silent.
From the hall a murmur as you stand
And look about, a question in your eyes.

Remember those who turned away in shame,
And then the twisted muscle in your face,
The jeering mouths, the prancing youth
Who then recited poem after poem:
About the new god too, the river
Rising as he received his laurels, the voices
After this in brooks and trees,
And in the north the steady rain that fell.

Something about Dionysius. It wasn't clear.
You'd swear this was the verse that you
Had sung before. Who knew about the mudbank?
How many galleys had passed by this year?
Why was there weeping in the city?
Who could have known about the poison in the drink?
The torches of the funerals burned all that day
Upon your eyes. I think they did say Plato,
But I cant be sure. It may have been Pythagoras.

It is the chance missed. Of course it's that.
Not all the other signs, not what was said
About a birthmark on your temple, the prophecy
About your mother, the sickness in the city,
Not one of these had mattered in the end.
It was the prize first, the fleece,
And then the wreck that followed.

Homage to Ezra Pound

(Mad, fascist and traitor in Italy)

I

So   of your sixty-three years   you
are an old man scrabbling verses
peevishly the old cantilations
are sung   in a cracked voice

in a dim room crouched on the floor
legs crossed   singing out the song
of laws   nor yet will they leave   you
alone

in the sixty-third year of your life

Votre age M'sieu Pound demands not
nor gives praise for the urn
the still vase within the vase that
moves   the porcelain that shines
even the image and most certainly

not for the youngest song of the lot
clothed in its vestments of Chinese
Persian   heraclitian   gold not praised
or even sung well in our time.

II

Except for me who pays homage
and I   I am bourgeoise and Jew
mad also as you are
                              by our time

is this not satisfaction enough
most subtle irony of all
I am of that darned clever bunch
who will say homage

even from the usurous lot
Shylocks clothed in a Shiffer-Hillman
or a one button roll taking
in my hands your songs
and asking the crowd to begin

III

For   Pound   we owe you the explanation
on a night I have seen ivory hands
curl and tap on the arms of chairs
I have seen Egyptian faces
and most prodigal of all these times
have seen
          islands   poets drowned   bridges

for twenty-six years allied myself
with the just cause
not enough for twenty-six years
begged a question of the time
of the crosslegged poets on floors
in asylums through three centuries
and a dozen continents

returned to the universal values
not enough for twenty-six years
also was among the armed
and the adventurous
went with the old prostitute
on her best time when her price

was much higher than the one she asked
of yours and you were on the other side
venting your spleen oh redbearded one
against myself

and it all came back to a table
with the man across saying
"you must accept all the facets of life
nor reject any part thereof"

IV

returned to singing the ivory hands
the egyptian face the body
which was so slow as a panther
returned to the female mind
in the dark whirlpool with its supple
and subtle turning slow and dear

sang with the mouth and the arms
and repeated the phrases
all things save the mystery of
the eyes repeated all things save
thy lips

asking was twenty-six years enough
for the praise of an urn and a regalia
for the clothes I give my songs
and yours   for the contempt
of the wrong so obviously
done not only to you but to our time
by those suffering from that wrong

the bourgeoise and the contented
trouble both mine and your thoughts
was it enough that of all the praises
after the insults there should only be
the one singing

for either your sixty-three or my
own twenty-six years

Horrible Workers—Rimbaud

Look on that pearl-edged city where
Dawn took you by the throat
And tell us now that Phoebe is a war,
Son of Horizons, whose verse is still a threat.

Now where you loved, that great assassination
Is gone good-sacred-hearted; neatly fashioned,
Now a pleasant seeing, fathoms above in a framed action,
Pearled to eternity; and all who are unvisioned

Are fashionable, see dawn in a cyclical glory
Like fish, or young chickens, or jellied things
As gleaming brains of men go by
Over the shore where your straddled shadow hangs.

It will be no effect of legends that
Those fall on your horizons, those eyes
That are abandoned engines, a soft hat,
A curled hand caressing a paper agony.

But without story though the day elapses,
Suns continuing, in a legendless land,
Horrible workers, we set out to your horizon of ellipses,
The unseen being of your eyed mind.

Husks of Things

For E.A.

Were he like the carapace,
Man could never run his race,
Armoured, brightly, to the hilt.
All this greenness, all this gilt,
Could claw Eden down, and track
Golden apples back and back,
To the time it dawned on Eve:
Spilt milk's not a thing to grieve
For.
    Remember:
            blame the ram,
And anyway, who cares a damn.
Fame is the spur no cock can know—
Or knight—or where the hens all go
After egging time is past.
Only food's the thing will last
From this dinnertime to that—
Or so it seemed from where he sat,
Musing on the ruin of race,
And the kindly carapace.

[I thought I had killed the revolution]

I thought I had killed the revolution
   with a proposition
   but a phrase leaped from the table
   and laying about with a word
left the headless committee
   in parts, like unpassed motions
   the amendments bleeding at their stumps.

Journal Poem

September, 1986, the poet defines himself,
his Canadian loyalties
   outside of himself (in America)
   outside of himself (in the Caribbean,
   an adjudicator for a Commonwealth
   Poetry Prize)
   (America—hyper-reality, an Italian
   definition by Umberto Eco)
   (Commonwealth)

The Canadian poet flees south in the fall,
brief stopover at Miami International Airport, and goes
on to Kingston, Jamaica.

I

Stroke

Bodily functions: Stroke July 1, 1986:
Canada Day: the world replaces itself by means of
a perceptual realignment.
So we all meet our own mortality
I didn't know it would be so difficult
only a poem, a new proprioception: location
of the extension of self in relation to space
but also subdural haematoma, the hard mother
(tr. Arabic) encasing the brain allows a small
blood seepage
hard mother. Relations between things
close by Dung cart
   Dungeon
   Dunghill
   Dungy
   Dunnage
   Dunstable
The world turns over south as north, East? West
Whenever there is a november in my soul

I seek out mild winters. Call me Ishmael
drawn to solipsistic pools
    dreaming south
The lullaby winds gentle soft evenings
Palms whispering
hallucinating
    Great God, the ship!
        the ship!
Allegory of body and soul
amid luxurious blossoming trees
Ataxia
    Pathological. Irregularities of animal
functions
    of the symptoms of disease
inability
    to co-ordinate voluntary movements
hence unbalanced. UnCanadian.
My left arm leaps out and salutes
an invisible officer.
Diplopic—an affection of the eyes in which
objects are seen as double.
    Hard mother
    The virtual image.
    (not really here)
Who is that lying at my feet?
The floor become the ceiling.
    This is not political.
We were taught by our last PM (Trudeau)
not to seek to
avoid revolution. The body turns over. Vertigo.
logically there is no one there
certainly not this colored body
this voluptuous woman.
this dreaming south.

Miami Vice: *Hyper-reality*

Taken by the word *International*,
He feels important,
   especially because the airport
is high-tech,
   the floor escalator
   takes us
   to an elevator that is a bus terminal
   announcing itself
   he becomes an international poet
arriving
   to seek out his luggage he must
   speak to security:
   a bulky southern policeman
who drawls
   "Sonny, we don't handle Toronto passengers
   only Dade County travelers"
   local once more
   two colored policemen
   they are everywhere
tell him
   "Sonny, where is your briefcase?"
   I left it here when I went to the phone.
   "It's not here now. *We* put it over there.
   Don't leave things unattended. This is
   An International Airport." They chuckle.
He sees T-shirts. 10,000 maybe. All inscribed
in the art deco mode. *Miami Vice*,
Has a beer at the art deco lounge neon-marked *lounge*,
Next *Miami Vice*, he sees
the study of a woman policeman
who loves a passing terrorist
of the IRA
   later blown up
   by his own illicit explosives.
He feels important. International.
The Canadian Vice

Kingston

Met at Kingston airport by Eddy Baugh,
professor of English of the University of West Indies,
Gentle colored.
   At Linguanea Club where he reserved a room for us.
Air conditioned. We met for dinner.
Under the trees. In the rich blooming garden.
He recalls a poem by Layton:
   "Anglo-Canadian"
   "A native of Kingston, Ont.
   Now his accent
   makes even Englishmen
   wince and feel
   unspeakably colonial."
The shredded remnant
of speech
and diction
All my wretched poetry still writing me
in the midst of these evasions
and all the denials.
   The Canadian Vice.

Published in *The Financial Post*, November 24, 1986

The Mermaid

      do the elements mingle in the sea
      or what words in the water
      could we say
                  woman
      whose hair lifts like the sun
      itself floating in the waves

      she is the sea's mild image
      her dolphin-mind

Message to Be Left in the Basement
Next to Mine Dug Last Sunday

not what you think; not thermonuclear
nor ice
        not insects nor the anger
of the god in whom we no longer
believe but the usual signs
of age
        the wet eyes (the CBC
news announcer blurred) the
loose groin and the pain
over the left back
            a crack
in the voice and diminished use
of
        also the weather is peculiar
        there has been no spring

        the teachers are not able
        to say literature is useless
        to those who chant the new songs

also if you do not look directly
        but slantwise you will see
        (some say headlights
        and great automobiles;
        some say the flash of
        horns and the black muscles
        of

there have been mailed men seen

and a corpulent poet who sailed here in
a bottle

Nervada: Nirvana

a spent afternoon
                    and light
twirling away like silver dollars
                    a desert
of clouds like cactus and
the red casino of the sun
flashing its neon
                    a last
turn of the wheel
                    before
a night darker than bourbon

who dreams of managing the sun

one loop of roulette to rope
its barbarous horses
                    and a ride
through a night where seven stars
twinkle like spots on the dice.

North-West Passage

We have sailed a thousand times into their fame.
No matter how we launch, or how implore,
Though the ship is always called a different name,
The breaking champagne bubbles are the same,
And it's always the same view of the dwindling shore.

A coastline never should be quite like this,
With such dull gulls, floating in the mind,
Voyaging should be terror, excitement, bliss,
Not a routine enchantment, with the hiss
Of flaccid water drifting out behind.

But that is how it is: *c'est la guerre,*
And say whatever else you choose to tell;
Only the gulls will hear you, in the dull air,
And certainly such gulls could not care,
And besides there is only the sea, and the fish smell.

There is only the sea—and that shrieking gull—
And, yes, the launching, and the dabbling foam:
And we're out on the waves, all sail and mast and hull,
And only the sky is flat and grey and dull,
And only we know whether we're going home.

Notes from the Diary of a Junior Executive

I suppose the grippe killed a few
    but the rest travelled in hordes
    and resisted it or colds or smallpox.

I saw them with the ravel of sweaters
    and coats from 1929 or string dresses
    the beads shaking and glittering
and their eyes glittering like the beads.

Somebody said it was 1412 and the cities
    were burning all along the coast
    that rape was common and the prows
    of their longboats in every harbour
peered over the church towers like dragons.

The Pope began to smell from his high fever
    something like Gordon's gin or cheap
    scotch or orange and bitters and rent
    shot sky high only a month before the crash.

Now Boast Thee Death

There were seene certaine fresh steppes or trackes
where it had gone on the tombe side toward the sea.
                                        (Plutarch)

The queen's robes, the confined breast, the girdled
thighs, upon a throne of senses, crowned by mind
and chambered with desire in the curtained tomb,
is offered him, a royal puzzle.
                                        Busily unties her life.
Tastes her, upon her nipple, on her arm. Her life
still warm as bourbon nurses him to drink,
it dangles from his bitings like an unwrapped knot.
He staggers with it past the ice-cube rocks,
the bourbon-coloured sea, the reeling planets.

Leaves tracks like tucks upon the blanket of the beach
sewing his seam to the venomous sea.

Nude

More dangerous than batons of emotion
twirling covered breasts of girls
like cubist nudes down staircased streets,
and fiercer than the midway thighs in beads
like nineteen-twenty living rooms stuffed
with Victorian chairs and bosomed ancient
aunts and boyish mothers strapped and flat
and hipless, these layers of oil lathered
to the inert planes of thought, the unconsuming
fire, the safe fire of colour.
                                        Still, momentous
as equations in a book of force, a torque
of thighs, it spins abstractions of its own
desires, quick black diagrams of a self
no longer bone but thought coloured
to the shape of bone or bone to shape
of flower.

Poem

Followed the lewd trains lurching to the city
The houses cringing, the blue smoke's frayed unwinding spools
The rail rackets shrieking nerve at close curve spills
Bemoaned the rocket's rabid gluttony of pity

Raged riot then. Turned snow storms inside out
Tore sunsets down and stuffed with hapless glee
The dark lane's garbage pail. Ran then to flout
At the rain red edge of cliffs the raving self
And with a great contempt, spit in the sea.

Raged useless until spent, crawled to a corner
From sudden heaving of the ground, and resting
Wretched, huddled there. Feared the storm growing
The plunging waves of paranoic winter.

Watched from a corner minutes, plucked and flung
With an insane leaping panic twisted, hurled
Bruising space in their mad path and wrong
And as a leaf in dying, inward curled:

Followed with aching eyes their cruel singing
Diminished. Their bright circles forever lost
Then lusted for them with the sobbing lust
Of one who seeks their sorrow clinging

Led to the sands of still, forgotten beaches
By the fall and swerve of a softly crying bird
Felt the quick stir and hope of warm wind reaches
Where anger fades and the waves' small consolance is heard.

Published in *The Students' Standard,* 30 March, 1946

Poem

Rain wets and rakes this fretted lawn of sky.
Today the sky is troubled by a clever scythe of wind
Where hawks, like paper, blown are trapped
In angry arcs and loops inside the sky.

So I shall take my troubled love and walk,
Watching the wind drive time before the clouds
Along the black crowd of rocks, into the stars,
Like glass, first mirror like water, like mica

On a rock, thrusting its queen's head, its regalia
Of foam at us. My love, Egypt is with us

While we walk and you are on a cliff
Clean blown by wind whom I would hold
Inside my anxious arms are Egypt's queen
And all your heraldry is dying once again.

The monumental palace, sphinx, rock built, face of man,
The sculptor's unbelievable knife facing the driving rain,

All structure, furrow of cheek and bone, breaking,
Rivulets and rivers on time to an incredible beach
Where like a forgotten pharaoh, dusted and blown
In his wrapped bandage of death, stand all kings
Directing the defense of sand castles in the tide.

A Poem about a Poem about a Poem

one afternoon
all the metaphors in the beehive
broke through their crusts of wax
and spilled over the busy bees
like honey
        stamen parts and pistils
twisted like the tongues of bees
and petals chewed by bee mouths
into balls of rag.
        At night
the similes which hung from trees
fell down into the grass
and ran across the lawns
toward the bee house.

the images bared their teeth
like dog-stars
        in his house
of lines and roots
an allegorist paced
observed his shadow
saw his tusks upon the wall.

Poems and Chorus from The Four Winds

For Mimi with all my love

I

A gull screams, winged back and bone
Flung over the wind's back, spray
Of blue-white feather in the rain;
By the sun, under the arch of sky
Sea-race foams, tides of blood roll
Over a hill and river. The arching bird,
The cry, contract into a hand's span,
A spinning sun, a dark eye.

II

As air is spirit so it shapes
The light cyclone of the weather,
Points, circular, the whirling vane,
The mild twisting cock, gathers
The moist sea in a dove-blue bosom
And parades its dragons, camels,
Castles in the sky.

The winds
Gather, the winds, directionless,
Come from their weathers, the winds
Together spin into the thin arena.

As air, light, shatters the leaves
And shadows, so seeds fall, so
Over the hill drifts the dazed feather,
The white spear burning like a sword,
And light air lifts the huge farm
And settles, featured like a garden,
Ground on the concrete city.

And air breathes men into clouds
Whose voice is thunder and whose smile

Lightens the country at four corners
Of the mapped tent, four bearded men:
I hear them breathing over the city,
Over the farm, over the hidden river.

III

Chorus of the Four Winds

East: Early, early in this man's life,
                     Across a land all water, a rivered land,
                     The streams flowing in the valley,
                     The simple cities planned,
                     Fresh and simple as rain, I ran.

South: Early, early in this man's life,
                     Under the hover of gulls,
                     Over the rib and arch of hills,
                     Heavy and feathered, I flew.

East: Early river, the whimper of water
                     In the basin

South: bed, nest, in the man's life

East: Green in the garden, my lady Eve,
                     He said, though I was male
                     Across the waste of snow

South: Out of the thoughtful mountains
                     Where the ice glows upon the shoulder
                     The cold peerless head

East: the flame
                     Upon the ice, the flame within the ice
                     That dances on the shattered ridge

Both Winds: Of mountain, bird, river, water,
                     Of fire, of ice, suddenly the garden

And summertime in this man's life:
What made the wheatfields glad and green
The thrifty bees to sing among the flowers
And the fresh plants to stand amid the falling rain

West: In summer when the rolling year
Wheeled stars across the summer sky,
Amid the stern processional of cloud
Into the day I stepped out of the sun
For whom the land pours gifts:
The brown torch burning in the marsh,
The purple rocket, vetch, the melting buttercup,
The flood of Iris, and the swollen stride of cattle,
Here spice, grape, oak, corn, honey,
The pointed wheat, and seldom seen, the prairie doe,
The hare, and all the summer long the voice
Of creaking earth rolled over on its hinge
Sung by the frog laid low into the drying mud.

Two Winds: Early, early in this man's life

West: Fire
Over the thoughtful mountains
Where the ice glows on the shoulder
The cold peerless head

Two Winds: Fire

West: The wheat bends, and the brown torch
Withers in its flame, and the one bee
Sings all day in the mouth of the Iris,
The sunflower bends. Out of the west

Two Winds: Fire

West: Dark on the dry earth the tanned skin lies
The core is rind, withered in the furrow
The black seed of the apple lies, the winds
Gather

North: Ice

Two Winds: Fire

Four Winds: Early, early in this man's life
              Something of this we knew before,
              How some would die in sloughs
              And some in rivers, how one would lie
              Tangled in the marshy weed,
              The river's mouth would crack,
              The black skin shrivel,
              Too early, the wheat not grown, the plant
              Dead, the root shrivelled in the earth.

Voice out of the Whirlwind:
              Out of the light and out of the dark,
              Out of the cloud, and out of the sun in the west,
              I spin. I am the dust. Bird, river,
              Ice, fire. Out of the furrow.
              Whoever planted me sees me grow.
              Early in this man's life
              I was the simple light, the spinning year,
              Let me dance over his grave.

June 1955

Pompilia

He said, "Now you can rest,
be quiet, listen to the geese."
I heard a dog growl once,
a strangled yelp.

                He said,
"These are trees, not hands,
no one leans upon the leaves,
the shadow is not blood."

He said, "Night shall come,
accept the mystery,
fall easily into sleep."

He said, "The sea is a cradle,
there will be no more drownings,
even the fish are kind."

I heard armies upon the beach
and saw the razor's tooth,
gleams that died with a death.

In dreams now, a broken wing
and large tree-hands,
two bleeding shadows,
a drowned dog cast on the beach.

Pompilia Outside Rome

I

If I said "hoopla" to the president
    or gargoyles of toothpaste
    or so much for redbrick,
    nothing so imperial

    or, feigning innocence,
    my own hands efficient
    with the keys to the safe

    after the plains burn
    after the summer of Vikings
    when the hordes have gone
    these monuments remain

do you think the walls would tumble down.
    No, I have seen archbishops
    lean as gothic cathedrals
    and a major louder than
    155mm artillery
              and I say
    these ruins remain

    only inside the poem
    I remarked the grey pouches
    hanging like moneybags
    and that his tongue
    green as a dollar bill
    was deflated
              depression
and whirlwinds over the pain

    when I stumbled from the office
    behind the math-chem-physics bldg
    the sun burned west Edmonton
    and the armies disappeared in smoke

II

grey eminence ruler of dust
a summer of plagues
  sun's shadow
  royal dust
 I pray for burned crops
 skeletons in our fields
 and the tentmakers journey

our youth in the desert
our cities dry
and the grasshopper
under the automobile wheel

Portrait of King David as Moses

In the clay oven where he worked
clay into brick he saw how flame
extorted whiteness from the glaze
that bricked him in. Therefore
he begged the flat egyptian girls
to fold him in their lunatic bright
ways.
       So much absurder than a loon
the cackle of this harpist startled
them. They burst, like moths, in flits
and sunders from his tomb, and left him
to his wrists and harping.

A deft god then taught him sleek
egyptian tricks, to don the hawk-
face, wear the beak of avarice,
and ply his strings in better trade
than bricking body in its simple
clay and mortar, so he begged
the Hebrew girls their crooked
favours for a wry and oriental
song.
       They therefore brought him
breasts of men long drowned
in reedy pools to hollo in,
and lenten lovers in their weeds
to pluck, and whips of upright men
to sting the tuneful flesh to harmony.

His deft taught wrist therefore extorts
his daily blood. His nightly cry,
absurder than a loon's, hollos
in ovens where the clay is glazed
by fire, where the brick on brick
shuts mortal owner in its simple shape.

Portrait of the Artist as Prairie

In the country of my words' two seasons
There are no others, but only a bare-boned
Winter child of a land, bent by time's rickets,
Crooked and thin as the sides of Alberta,
His slattern mother, and the twin ghost of him
Solid and golden as a wheat grain in a good summer.

In my country's language the two children ride
Forever Siamese and mirror the same pony words of wishes.
By the river where the one goes on his horse of desire
The other goes along, a centaur of a boy in water:
And plump and silver the bare-boned child of winter
Sees in the water the stars of Sheriffs and spends
His bullet nouns to kill the villain time and prison.

In my land's language he begs for penny words
Where speech is not rich and is not spent as silver
But grudgingly given a copper few words at a time
The bronze of admonition, or hard as northern nickel
The hand hoarded language is passed from mouth to mouth.

And in my country's frost speech must be spent for reason
Not toys but ticks of words to cover and to measure
With the odd cross word of rhyme
The quilt and blanket for the forest of time
And those who breathe in ghosts of it
Save speech for the payment of the spirit.

But in my country's time is a summer of language
And a rain of words over the year gulleyed plains
Where stream the furious rivers of sentences
And spills a water of language over the child
There pike-furious for language and fish silver
In the spending of it rides the ghost of the bare boned child
Plump and smiling, stalking child miles over the land
And as the watery rider, part of his golden stallion
Oh on the horizon he flashes flesh past time
To the thunder of hooves in the clouds of fable.

Prologue

Nudity of manner was well thought of,
and stripped desire showed her breast,
the inner pose exposed itself in colour
squeezing gobs of sun and ungowned moon
upon the canvas of our eyes.
                              Shape-makers
holidayed in bronze and stone whole festivals
of motion, passion of the circling arm,
and merriment of pelvis in the park.
There was much wrist-wresting and voices,
metaphor-makers were in great demand,
and forgers of fiction.
                              Through the land
the unstalked animals walked in pairs
to naming booths.

The Rape of Europa

whatever has been said: it is the absolute protest
            the soul hung in its soot
            shrieks about ugliness

you've no idea about the irrationalities of poetry
I said to my physicist who was examining a mote
in my eye

            though I have been blind for years
            and suffered cataracts of tears
            to wash away this dust

            once I saw

a bull-white sun lift upon his slender horns
the great white cow of the sky

            and bleed away her lust.

Reactionary Song

On our bodies' prosper, the declension of worms
Constructs a new generation, the colour informs,
The crabbed monkey colour which our agony warms.

Delicate as a Japanese print
The Emperors go sailing
In a three ring pattern of stunt
And wailing.

With a magician's instinct for disappearance
And the miracle return,
With the confidence of sailors in appearance,
And the mortician's concern,
They bury us often.

And the new rulers soften
At the light of the horizon in the dawn;
Like a hungry generation they gnaw at the sky
Where the obvious assurance of the sun
That last cherry of evening hangs
On its lips like a lark and a song.

Forever at such altars we light our candles
Between those lands where the currents run too fast
For medial sails we hopefully erect and handle,
Or voyages begun by an auspicious feast.

And grief upon us in an evening rhyme
With shriek on shriek in darkness, drops,
Like the flapping of crows fed too long on Carrion Time.

But the dead atlas continues to support the world
With his forgotten skeleton, an architectural reflex.

A Refusal

the only sin
the sin *against* the body
refusing it
              why then
how deeply I have sinned
to love your wide gaze
as if it were of paradise
of loves unheard undreamed
of gods who knew not love
as we know love
                      hairy
greek men their moustache
greedy for your hair
are right I'd say are all
that ought to be those goats

listen exec blue stocking 63
I sin by loving your wide eyes
as if they gazed to paradise

as if you didnt know
as if you didnt yearn

when I'd be wise unnatural
and tell you in my voice and vice
of high spiritual things
to think you innocent
whose innocence was love

I wish all you'd looked for
those gone fixed years ago
I think your eyes were looking
for as if you saw doves, loves
gods knew nothing of rapists
or of blind Moroccan eyes
sewn shut or whatever they
do about flies and bugs and things

I wish that dull picture-making
man hadnt fixed you in that gaze
I remember anyhow in my class
when you accepted my own guilt
as if that were
                        well what use
saying now that it was innocence
I loved when it is innocence
my love would take away just
as the rapist on some island
seeing your violent love violate
or some Lebanese lusting for you
took gratuitously whatever he could

Remembrance of Things Past

... after the stories
    after the campfires
    and the stories
stumbling into the daylight
    knowing about sun
    about the trees
    about the gopher
nothing of my people
    the stories dwindling
    like stars in the dawn
    only the storyless sun
      and the desert stumps

who was whispering
    about peril
who about
    journeys
who told us
    in the evening
    by the flowering stars
    by the robed trees

before the rodent sun
    before the teeth
    of the storyless sun
    before the bare stars

    wordless
      the yellow gophers

Scholars

Bald heads, we
(Yeats said) respectably
Edit and annotate
And uncreate:

Assemble bits,
Devise designs,
Bemuse our wits
Emending lines

(Said he) for this
Have poets rhymed—
For spectral kiss
Grotesquely mimed.

Bald heads, we,
With him, respectably
Expostulate, hesitate,
Read on—and annotate.

Science Fiction

The last man, his great rod in his hand,
crept to the moronic wife who mumbled charms
over the coals that glowed with (numbers here)
and in the rouge of creation (cosmetic for the
lips singing: the croon of dead children)
I saw these prairie images: furnace, and wind
    over the coals, over the hot coal sun.

Second Part of an Unfinished Moral Dialogue

You have taken my name (continued)
  the lawyer with the icy teeth
  and the frostbitten smile

He held the icicle under my nose, waved
the stick forbiddingly
      Admit your part
in this general frost, he persisted (the judge
ordered a retraction and the left flank moved
back, exposing the wrecked city
         bare breasted
women threatened me, recoiled from me, held
bodies (children's) like flags before me)

You were seen sowing teeth under the moon

  (fully armed the teeth sprang up, armed
  like the ocean, the wheat bent under the sun,
  the dog barked beside the sun: a cock crew
  fanned its tail in a bravado)

        At this
I sprang out of my fleece, shook golden
fingers: general astonishment, applause.

I have friends in the cave I said
not unwittily, and I wanted neither girls
nor jewels. I want the paint taken off.
I want my eyes to see again what used to be,
my friends melted, sent out of the icy cave,
no wars, inscriptions unwritten again,
the children restored.
      The judge stroked
a cloudy moustache (storms) adjusted glasses
(burning cities): I thought he snarled.

The law is pathetic, he said.

Several Other Ways of Getting at the Same Thing

as you say: there we are
there: meaning a loaf or half?
or even the yeast
or simply yesterday
when I was half-baked
in the oven of your burning eyes?

you say: ah yes, so it is
it is: it, the splendour of it
careening like a planet
settles on blown fly-paper
and those spindly stuck legs
pointing north-east and south-west
toward the giant IS of glue and sand

let us be true to one another

true is the it: a planetary beach
    some shadow
             you know the rest

Stroke

Some children shrieked at hopscotch that spring morning
I stooped for a soft beachball at my feet.
A sharp stab in my eye was the first warning:
the purple skyline wavered in the heat.
As the blaring ambulance blurred the landscape, I
lay helpless, my entire right side gone dead.
My mind buzzed round in circles like a fly.
I tried to speak, but my jaw sank like lead.
They fed and bathed and shat me all of June.
One day they told me I'd be walking soon.
I snorted. I'm afraid to go outside,
scared stiff of evenings when old friends drop round:
a minute portion of my brain has died,
I hear Apocalypse in every sound.

Talkative Poem

This is the poem I'll confront directly:
it has said too much.
It has been indiscreet.
It betrayed my friends
and angered and hurt my wife.
How shall I ever silence it?

Do you have no agreement with me
about the nature of honesty?
Do you think anything is permissible?
What shall I do later
when you have written all love out of my life?
Turned me into stone? A noted gossiper?
How shall I live with my silences then?
Or is that your intent?
Finally to silence me?
In the end to live
in your own inscrutability
no longer understood, no longer heard,
known only for your hardness

That Other Time of Year

(set to an old tune)

And I swore we'd out for summer,
Out beyond the farthest bay,
Where the sun strikes hot on morning
And the great gulls greet the day;

Where the fish-stink sands are yellow,
And the water blue as pie:
O I never thought we'd wander
Round the cliff-top till we die.

Yet all scarp and boulder memories
Lacerate the mind, and we,
Running naked on the beaches,
Glance the headland to the sea.

And we never stop to wonder
About swimming's sin or joy,
While the surf is hissing landward,
In to bell the tossing buoy.

O think not that the ocean
Has a bed as good for you
As it had for Captain Ahab
And that damned big white whale, too.

We cannot all be part of myth,
That's reserved for very few,
Gravestone, cromlech, monolith,
Or memory may have to do.

But we all are part of sunlight
And the air which runs as free,
Up the sloping shores to morning,
As the salmon-sprawling sea:

For the sea-shell beaches stretching
Out beyond the farthest bay,
Can but tell the eager swimmers
All they know of summer's day.

Tithonus

To EWM who, being given immortality, turned into a grasshopper.

Scrape, scrape. Well, spindle-shank,
Thou wast not born for death, immortal bore,
And still you rub your belly and you ache for music.

What would you hatch, bald patch?
Another bowl of farmers' plagues for hungry generations?
A year, perhaps, of cities and its moan:
Suburban basements
                            opening on the loam
Of parlous ease in prairie lands forlorn?

To Certain Poets Who Spoke of Vision

Of poetry they know some, more than I
Of how it comes unmused, unbidden:
Words are exhaled from them like a sigh.
They stand knee deep in words while I
Swim in a sea of words and hidden

Half in water, half in air, look back
Into the sea of me and see my arms
My legs, broken by that film of black
And ugly water, turn upon my back
And float a while, safely in a sea of harms.

Tower of Babel

When flood, fire, fever overthrow
This city and the ones I love in it
I dont know that I'll weep for them
Though I might for a minute.

I can despair now.
This seems the time for grief
Before the final hour
When timidities beyond belief
Assemble Babel's tower

And everyone climbs on it
Speaking a language I do not know
Though sometimes when I'm brief
Enough and when I climb with them
I think that I invented it.

Trio in Brass and Season

For Canadian Poets

First Male Figure
O he was shipwrecked in the snow.
Where no ships went he died to go;
Ghost of a fop, pirating the blood
Of paradise; to be a nun's priest
He priest-like was who was impressed
In service of dead kings, to sail the flood
And perjure woman's vanity, and lie, and loot,
And beat his sister's squire, and plot
A fiendish victory against the wholly unreal lot.

Second Male Figure
From unalterable wit of rain
He bailed out a new season of voices
For every fashion—but always
His sad short sturdy stern
Dragged in a current of poems;
Prow up, a whisker of foam
Curled on his fair face,
And his heavy rudder
Turned to a shore
Where sanded on a broad beach
Splayfoot, paddled among, gulls,
Their unbelievable songs.

Female Figure
In fog no less than they she forced to sail
The paper ships but on a deadly sea
She launched atlantic up a graceful wail
Full of the wilting schooners; O wickedly
As they went down
She wept her living tears
To see the paper sailors drown.

Chorus of Unreal Voices
  Unholy trio cast in greening brass
  Wept by the weather, topped by formless snow,
  Accept our laurels, crown your eyes of glass,
  Who watched, still, glazed, a frozen time ago.
  O you are clasped by elementary calm
  In caves of light, statued on those bases, there
  Vaulted to innocence, moulding through a psalm
  Of years, a cluttered green attitude, a form
  Of all our judges, piercing through the glare
  Of sunlight, perpetual in the public square.

Variation on Levertov's Peppertrees

I don't even remember if lemon
   comes into the poem
   yet think of nipple-shapes
   while a merry jaundice swims
   over the orange landscape

not quite a sunrise
this sandy syrup SUNUP

but why then peppertrees?

Ah, I do have a taste of truth
  (a dog followed by a daub
  followed by a dog, another daub
  and a semi-nude body, three
  slashes of broad yellow paint)
  out of dear old President Stevens'
  symposia: order's the thing

YOU say the tree's gone then
there's no tree among daubs and dogs
but you have forgotten me
and where I sit among the leaves
having got there
             oh yes there
is where I have excellently
gotten to
         to be a pallette
in the tree or (don't think
I miss your sly objection—
questions curl their tails
around all singing boughs
and swarm among the daubs and dogs)
is it a tree in a pallette?

Palatable and palpable
the tree-bird-song
the lemon evening
dogs and the sun-drop
a nipple on the bosom of the day

The Wizardry of Is

arrived
     by no means known but by skills
     of craftsmanship, of-pity too,
     the dogwork
         and found only
the blunt stupidity of thorny trees
harrowing
     this one like a hurt boy
limping across the yard, and this one,
crippled, his sly hand thrust into my
eye, singing of salvation, the sky
crumpled like an accordion with a moan.

so they scuttled my quest like a Q boat
in 1914 and I roamed for a while in no
man's land, looking at pictures, the face
of pasty fear, the ace of speedboat land,
the marquis of speed.
        Everything comes
of a seed, I said to my wife, the flower,
the child, and everything ends in a seed,
the lion floating on our lawn, the tigerish
sun who is planted in earth every night.

Young Man Addresses His Love

The punishment we deliver
Under a silver moon
In spite of all our laughter
Is a comic paper

The peculiar present sin.
Our eyes cup delicately
And admiring lips sip after
Tea garden praises for the daring
Of darling centaurs and a softer
White lady on a horse
Wearing her silver smile.

I have loved you better
For all my soul than words
But Time is no nectar
And the honeyless passion
No flower the bee sways towards.

I would be out of time and fashion
In famous iron the nun sorrow
Of your face, but religion's
No honey, and the bee's at Tomorrow.

And disaster, a mild Claudius,
Pours poison tea in our ears,
Whispering sin in our faces.

All move in the moonlight
Until in Time's flower,
Star, centaur, and lady,
And every white horse is a tear.

Zenith: Saving to Disk

This poem will be saved
a saved poem can not be made up out
of lines that will not remain
invisible or words that wont
dissolve—the illusion will
at last become the reality

or will it become real because
it has become print and not
these ghostly flickering
figures on a screen

figures on a screen
illusions dreams
of words dreamt by me:

the absence of my self
the absent self who writes
the ghostly writing self

the ghost writer

dreaming his own holocaust
himself the victim and his own
executioner

[Computer poem on Zenith 148, Draft Three]

NOTES to VOLUME 2

[Editors' comments in brackets.]
Mandel's comments indented.

Third Person Singular

[Mandel, with Esther Gudjonson and Antony Thorne—the other poets whose work appeared here—wrote a Foreword to the volume:]

> This work presents song and lyric as in poetry and has as its subjects those things which are the rightful subjects of song and lyric. It is not designed as wisdom or reason or logic but rather to fulfill the use of poetry as we see it, which is certainly, if nothing else the presentation of human experience in an organized form. The meaning of our work lies in that as well as in any statement or theme applicable to the poems.
>
> These poems are in the tradition of modern American and English poetry, reflecting the cosmopolitan view, related in some small extent to the metaphysical poetry of today but they are primarily romantic in spirit and treatment. As such they represent the view that reality is achieved and understood by the individual as a creative being. They emphasize those aspects of reality which adhere to the individual in isolation as well as his social context.
>
> The romantic in poetry believes that the individual will succeed, if he can, only by his understanding of those things which are closest to him as an individual; such things being love, death, the desire and need for communication and the search for faith. If his poetry or any poetry has a public function (which we believe it has) this is the function; poetry brings understanding or belief in those things. Because it is song or lyric or poetry, people go to it; otherwise it fails, both in purpose and as poetry.

Crusoe

[Dedication: "This is for Peggy and Dennis / in the dark wood, a way."]

Dreaming Backwards [Initial title: *The Blue Men of Saskatchewan*]

[Dedication: "To Eva, my mother, and to all my fathers." Mandel was fascinated with ancestral memory. His parents emigrated to Canada from the Ukraine. His father, Charles Mandel (1893-1956), was born near Kiev. His mother, Eva (Berner) Mandel (1898-1955), was born in Odessa. "(T)o all my fathers..." refers to the poets of the English tradition. In the mid-1980s, Mandel visited the Ukraine, the area around Kiev, looking for the village where his father had been born. He was informed, on mentioning the name of the village to a guide, that "hundreds" of places bore that name. For Mandel, the dedication was an acknowledgement of a plurality of fathers; the anecdote suggests diaspora, the scattering/multiplication/refraction of the father's name, which, to be Freudian, is also linked to images of the feminine.]

Uncollected/Unpublished Poems

Cabbages and Trees [Alternate title: "Cost of Living"]

The Mermaid

> There was a glorious painting of a sunflower in that room where I wrote the poems: against a gold-red background a most curious flower, with a gold-red centre and a white collar. And oddly a line from *Moby Dick* kept running through my mind: "the meaning of that story of Narcissus, who because he could not grasp the tormenting mild image he saw in the fountain, plunged into it and was drowned. But that same image we ourselves see in all rivers and oceans. It is the image of the ungraspable phantom of life; and this is the key to it all." (I always type id, by the way, instead of is).

Portrait of King David as Moses. [Initial title: "Masochist."]

Tower of Babel

[Alternate version of third stanza: "Which rises downward / Like a dim reflection."]

The Wizardry of Is

> I don't know where the images of this one originate, but they are also film-images, montages.

Zenith: Saving to Disk

> Computer Poem on Zenith 148/Draft three.

[In the mid-1980s, Mandel experimented with "computer poems," intrigued by the possibility of letters as "not real...not really there...illusions."]

INDEX OF FIRST LINES OF POEMS

Page numbers from Volume 1 in regular type (pages 1-433).
Page numbers from Volume 2 in boldface type (pages 443-737).

INDEX OF POEM TITLES

Page numbers from Volume 1 in regular type (pages 1-433).
Page numbers from Volume 2 in boldface type (pages 443-737).